GENDER TRENDS
IN SOUTHEAST ASIA

GENDER TRENDS
IN SOUTHEAST ASIA

Women Now, Women in the Future

EDITED BY

THERESA W. DEVASAHAYAM

LSEAS

INSTITUTE OF SOUTHEAST ASIAN STUDIES
Singapore

First published in Singapore in 2009 by ISEAS Publishing
Institute of Southeast Asian Studies
30 Heng Mui Keng Terrace
Pasir Panjang
Singapore 119614

E-mail: publish@iseas.edu.sg
Website: http://bookshop.iseas.edu.sg

The responsibility for facts and opinions in this publication rests exclusively with the authors and their interpretations do not necessarily reflect the views or the policy of the publisher or its supporters.

ISEAS Library Cataloguing-in-Publication Data

Gender Trends in Southeast Asia : women now, women in the future / edited by Theresa W. Devasahayam.
    Papers presented at the Symposium on Gender Trends in Southeast Asia, Singapore, 4 December 2008.
    1.   Women—Southeast Asia—Congresses.
    I.   Devasahayam, Theresa.
    II. Symposium on Gender Trends in Southeast Asia (2008 : Singapore).
HQ1745.8 G32   2009

ISBN 978-981-230-955-6 (hard cover)
ISBN 978-981-230-956-3 (PDF)

Typeset by International Typesetters Pte Ltd
Printed in Singapore by Utopia Press Pte Ltd

CONTENTS

CONTRIBUTORS

Theresa W. Devasahayam is Fellow and Gender Studies Programme Coordinator at the Institute of Southeast Asian Studies, Singapore.

Gavin W. Jones holds a joint appointment in the National University of Singapore, as Professor and Research Team Leader in the Asia Research Institute, and as Professor in the Department of Sociology, Faculty of Arts and Social Sciences.

Bernadette P. Resurreccion is Lecturer at the Asian Institute of Technology, Bangkok, Thailand.

Susan Blackburn is Associate Professor in the School of Political and Social Inquiry at Monash University, Melbourne.

Rashidah Shuib is Professor and Director of the Women's Development Research Centre, Universiti Sains Malaysia, Malaysia.

Maznah Mohamad is Visiting Senior Fellow at the Asia Research Institute and the Department of Malay Studies, National University of Singapore.

LIST OF TABLES AND FIGURES

Tables

Figures

FOREWORD

"Gender Trends in Southeast Asia: Women Now, Women in the Future" was a symposium held on 4 December 2008 in conjunction with the Gender Studies Programme of the Institute of Southeast Asian Studies. Established in 2005, the Programme seeks to explore how gender inequality plays out in the Southeast Asian region. More specifically, the Programme examines two broad areas: (a) wo(men) and politics, and (b) the health and social concerns of vulnerable women including sex workers, trafficked women, internally displaced women, low-skilled migrant women workers, and poor women independently heading households. The objective of the Programme is to emphasize two points: (a) that gender is a field worthy of rigorous study because a gender perspective is critical to give voice to women, and (b) that ISEAS undertakes research in several emerging concerns related to women in the region.

Why the focus on women's issues is a justifiable question. Since women make up half of the world's population, research and analysis on women is critical in understanding one of many forms of social stratification. Undoubtedly women face unique disadvantages and, in turn, social problems because of their gender identity. Hence in some contexts, it becomes important to formulate policies informed by critical debate to ensure that women are not left behind and that they share in the fruits of development equally with men. For these reasons and many others, the trends and changes in women's lives and the obstacles women face in advancement and securing their own rights are worthy of research, documentation and analysis.

The recent symposium provided a platform for discussion of various issues related to women in contemporary Southeast Asia. Since the symposium was the first in the series on "Gender Trends in Southeast Asia", the speakers' presentations covered a broad range of topics: (a) women and family; (b) women and employment; (c) women and politics; (d) women and health; and (e) women and religion.

This volume is a compilation of the papers presented at the symposium. There are three aims in putting together this publication. First, it provides a written documentation of some current concerns of Southeast Asian women. Second, the publication serves to aid policy-makers, academics and NGOs working on gender issues in the region to recognize the disadvantages and problems faced by Southeast Asian women. Third, this volume will enable policy-makers, academics and women's NGOs to track periodically the changes and continuities experienced by women in this region.

The Institute under its Gender Studies Programme, coordinated by Dr Theresa W. Devasahayam, strives to increase understanding of how gender inequality is expressed and perpetuated in different domains. The symposium held this year focused on a range of issues related to women in Southeast Asia. It is hoped that with each symposium, our understanding of these issues will increase.

Ambassador K. Kesavapany
Director, Institute of Southeast Asian Studies
Singapore
15 January 2009

MESSAGE

MRS YU-FOO YEE SHOON, MINISTER OF STATE FOR COMMUNITY DEVELOPMENT, YOUTH AND SPORTS

Thank you for giving me the opportunity to address you on a subject that has always been of special interest to me. I find each day of my work fulfilling as I am directly involved in advancing the interests of women in Singapore and things that women traditionally care a lot about, like family, children, marriage, parenting and even what women want men to do more of!

Politics

It is important to empower women to participate in decision-making at the community and national levels. The Singapore Government welcomes women to leadership positions based on meritocracy. In the domain of politics, for example, female representation in the Singapore Parliament has been increasing. Women make up 24.5 per cent of the Singapore Parliament today. This percentage exceeds the Inter-Parliamentary Union's world average of 18.3 per cent.[1]

The number of women holding public office has increased, especially in local government, at the higher levels of political participation. For example, women in Lao PDR, Timor-Leste and Vietnam have prided themselves in holding more than 25 per cent of national parliamentary seats in 2007. Other Southeast Asian countries have between eight and 16 per cent of seats held by women in national parliament.[2]

Employment

As gender equality is the goal adopted by the international community and national governments, people's rights, responsibilities, social status and access to resources should not depend on their gender. This includes employment opportunities for women as well as men.

According to the internationally agreed commitments under the International Labour Organization (or ILO), some key international labour conventions for gender equality include: discrimination in employment, equal remuneration, workers with family responsibilities and maternity protection. The ILO reports that in 2006, the female labour force participation rate (or LFPR) is lower than males in all the countries covered. Vietnam and Thailand has the highest LFPR at 72 and 66 per cent respectively. In comparison, the rate for other Southeast Asian countries are below or around 50 per cent.

In Singapore, the LFPR was 78 per cent for males and 54 per cent for females in 2007. Although top positions in the public and private sectors used to be traditionally male-dominated, it is no longer the case. In recent years, we have witnessed the rise of many Singapore women to these very positions, attesting to the rise of women's influence in the nation. 47 per cent of Singaporean women were in the professional, managerial or technical positions in 2007, compared to 50 per cent for men. I am pleased to see that the proportion of female employers have increased from 20.1 per cent in 2003 to 23.1 per cent in 2007.

In Singapore, the Government is committed to equal remuneration and treatment for work of equal value. We ratified a key ILO Convention on equal remuneration in 2002. The median monthly income for full-time employed females in Singapore last year was 87 per cent that of males. It was 81.3 per cent a decade ago.[3] Apart from Singapore, seven other Southeast Asian countries have ratified that Convention,[4] with the exclusion of Brunei, Myanmar and Timor-Leste.

Fertility Concerns

In recent years, there are women in Southeast Asia who have made great strides especially in the more developed economies in the region. Especially among the growing number of educated women, careers have taken priority and this has led to smaller family sizes and, consequently, a falling fertility rate — a pressing concern for some governments, including Singapore. According to the World Fertility Patterns 2007, the world's fertility rate is 2.6. Of the

11 Southeast Asian countries, Singapore has the lowest total fertility rate at 1.3, followed by Vietnam at 1.9. The highest are Timor-Leste and Laos with a fertility rate of 4.7 and 4.6 respectively.[5]

Health

In the area of health, women suffer greater vulnerabilities than men. Women much earlier on in life face reproductive health problems. The battle against breast cancer is increasing following the trends in many developed countries. Every year, some 1,300 women in Singapore are diagnosed with breast cancer, adding to the increasing pool of women diagnosed with breast cancer here. Breast cancer rates have increased by about 25 per cent in the last ten years[6] in Singapore.

In the less developed Southeast Asian countries, maternal mortality continues to record staggering high numbers because of poor access to good pre-natal and post-natal gynecological healthcare. For example in Timor-Leste, it is estimated that the maternal mortality rate is up to 660 for every 100,000 live births. We are fortunate that the rate is six in 100,000 in Singapore.[7]

Education

Education represents the most sustainable solution to level the playing field between different groups in society. In fact, one of the eight Millennium Development Goals committed by the United Nations is to achieve universal primary education by 2015. According to the United Nations Children's Fund (or Unicef) report in 2007, 115 million children of primary school age do not attend school, and 53 per cent are girls.

The world literacy rates for youths (or those aged between 15 to 24) from 2000 to 2006 for males and females are 91 and 85 per cent respectively. In general, the youth literacy rates for both genders in Southeast Asian countries are comparable and higher than the world average, with the exception of Cambodia and Lao PDR.[8] In Singapore, both girls and boys have equal access to quality education from young, and the youth literacy rate is 99 per cent for both genders.

Though women in some Southeast Asian countries may have lower literacy rates than men, I note that a "new gender gap" has emerged in the newly developing countries in the region. For instance, in Brunei, Malaysia, Thailand, Philippines and also Singapore, enrollment at the tertiary education institutions among females has been higher than males. The higher proportion of females in higher education has been said to have led to the flourishing of a range of non-governmental organizations focused on women's issues since the 1980s that have advocated women's equality in various arenas.

Conclusion

The symposium "Gender Trends in Southeast Asia" organized by the Institute of Southeast Asian Studies will inform us further on the current trends related to women in this region — the progress they have made in the different spheres and the obstacles they continue to face in achieving equal status to men.

Women's empowerment and advancement in all spheres of life are crucial for the progress of society. To enable women to harmonize their multiple obligations to work and family, women need a total supportive approach encompassing policies, services and mindset change of the individual, family, employers, and the community.

The fact that all Southeast Asian countries have signed the Convention on the Elimination of All Forms of Discrimination Against Women demonstrates the commitment of governments in the region to advance and promote gender equality.

With increasing emphasis on enhancing the status and progress of women on each national government's agenda, I have every confidence that women in Southeast Asia can look towards a more promising future.

With that, I wish all of you a fruitful symposium. Thank you.

Notes

1. Source <http://www.ipu.org>.
2. Source <http://www.adb.org/Documents/Books/Key_Indicators/2008/pdf/Goal-03.pdf>.
3. Source: Ministry of Manpower.
4. Source <http://www.ilo.org/ilolex/english/newratframeE.htm>.
5. Source <http://www.un.org/esa/population/publications/worldfertility2007/worldfertility2007.htm>.
6. Source: Ministry of Health.
7. Source: UNICEF. The reported maternal mortality rate from 2000 to 2006 is 6.
8. Cambodia: 88 and 79 per cent for males and females respectively; Lao PDR: 83 and 75 per cent respectively.

ACKNOWLEDGEMENTS

This book is a compilation of the papers presented at the one-day symposium "Gender Trends in Southeast Asia: Women Now, Women in the Future" organized by the Institute of Southeast Asian Studies on 4 December 2008. The symposium is an activity of the Gender Studies Programme at the Institute.

We would like to express our gratitude to Konrad Ardenauer Stiftung (KAS) for making the symposium as well as this publication possible. The funding received from KAS is a testament to its commitment to the study of women's experiences, interests and concerns in Southeast Asia.

We would also like to express our thanks to the National Committee for UNIFEM, Singapore for co-partnering with ISEAS in publicizing the symposium.

Introduction

WOMEN IN SOUTHEAST ASIA: CHANGES AND CONTINUITIES

Theresa W. Devasahayam

Southeast Asia as a region has undergone vast economic and social transformations in the last several decades. Women as a collective have seen their lives changed as a result of rapid development and economic growth. The Human Development Index records higher levels of literacy and primary school enrolment rates, and increases in life expectancy in most parts of the world, including countries in Southeast Asia, compared to a decade ago (Human Development Report 2006). The Philippines is a notable example in the region having closed the gender gaps in both education and health, joining a list of ten countries in the world with similar achievements (The Global Gender Gap Report 2008).

In the face of rapid economic and social change, it is important to ask how women and men have fared especially since women's interests and concerns differ from those of men. This leads to other questions related to the progress of the sexes: (a) In what areas have women been able to achieve parity with men?; (b) In what areas do women encounter specific disadvantages based on their gender as compared with men?; and, (c) How have women's concerns and problems been addressed by governments in this region with the aim of encouraging gender equality? In responding to these questions, it is important first and foremost to contextualize Southeast Asian women's experiences within the larger cultural and historical framework particular to this region.

1

The position that indigenous Southeast Asian women enjoy a relative autonomy has long been in the centre of debate in academic circles. Assertions have been made that women in this region have stood apart from their sisters in the rest of Asia by way of the relatively high level of autonomy they possess (Stoler 1977; Strange 1981; Atkinson and Errington 1990). Scholars have singled out a number of factors for the autonomy of women in the region. For one, Southeast Asia, they argue, has been characterized by both bilateral and matrilineal kinship systems, with the exception of Vietnam, unlike in East Asia and many parts of South Asia where patrilineal kinship systems tend to dominate (Dube 1997). Hutheesing (1994, p. 342) elaborates on this point:

> Observers of Southeast Asian countries have been impressed by the incidence of female independence and exercise of authority. Given this set of circumstances, Southeast Asia would represent a variant model of gender which stands in contrast to the patrilineal systems with their link to formalised political power in the Chinese tradition and the corporate caste groupings of India ... clearly built into the structures.

Daughters are also highly valued and not perceived to be a financial burden on the family. The relatively high autonomy possessed by women is also captured in residence patterns: in many Southeast Asian communities, married couples often have the flexibility of living with or near the wife's parents, thus reflecting the important function played by maternal relatives (Jamilah 1992; Medina 2001). Within the household, women's responsibility goes beyond the role of caregiver/nurturer; men transferred their earnings to their wives who controlled and allocated the household budget (Li 1989; Sullivan 1994).

Besides, the range of functions women held outside the household presented themselves as self-supporting individuals on par with the autonomous male. One of the most striking examples of Southeast Asian women's autonomy is their significant engagement in economic activity. Women's presence in the village markets is strong and their earnings as entrepreneurs are critical to the survival of the family (Alexander and Alexander 2001). In the labour sector especially in agriculture, the contribution of women has long been indispensable.[1] In matters of property relations, women also enjoy a distinct advantage. Moreover in the region, women took on prominent roles in indigenous religious rituals as much as men: they were shamans who engaged in exorcism, spiritual healing, agricultural magic and so forth (Hay 2005). The power Southeast Asian women held was also demonstrated in their skills in managing ceremonial feasts, and the organization of labour and credit societies as well.

Wazir (1995, p. 16) explains the importance of looking at how gender is constructed on a day-to-day level in the Southeast Asian region *vis-à-vis* the Western paradigm:

> The assumption that one should begin with the premise of unequal power generating gender hierarchies is not necessarily relevant in non-Western civilisations in Southeast Asia, which derive a theory of knowledge from concepts and values of bilateralism: the need to maintain social relationships through rules of complementarity and similarity rather than hierarchy and opposition, and the need to reduce imbalances in power through mutual responsibility and cooperation rather than oppression and force.

Wazir's (1995) argument, thus, is that the premise of unequal power generating gender hierarchies found in Western societies may not necessarily be relevant to Southeast Asia. In this region, concepts and values of bilaterality, emphasising complementarity and similarity rather than hierarchy and opposition, are of central significance in shaping and directing social behaviour.

This is not to say that women do not suffer disadvantages. An area in which women suffer a clear disadvantage is in initiating a divorce (Stivens 1996). The instances in which women face considerable gender inequality, however, are when they come up against heavily male-dominated structures presented by Islam (Wazir 1992). When entangled in these instances, women conduct themselves in recognized ways within the informal structures of the local cultures to retain their autonomy (Wazir 1995).

But if other semblances of gender inequality are found in the region, colonialism has been singled out to be another underlying factor for the emerging stratification between men and women. Colonial regimes propagated patriarchy and diminished the power held by women by "rewriting" customary laws. In some areas, women were recruited as cheap wage labourers in the tea, sugar, tobacco and rubber plantations and in processing factories managed by the colonial powers. Wage rates were also set at two-thirds that of men's, thereby encouraging differences between the sexes (Alexander and Alexander 2001). Nonetheless, women remained influential in community life with segments of the female population playing a crucial role in leading anti-colonial rebellions. Particularly educated women were in the forefront of fighting patriarchy and confronting gender inequality and oppression

(Zohra and Nurul 2000); it was this group of women who had been exposed to feminist ideas and saw the necessity to change the course of their destiny (Ford 2002; Ng, Maznah, and tan 2006).

In addition to colonialism, globalization and neo-liberalism, following the rise of the nation-state in Southeast Asia, have been identified as two other factors that have further accentuated gender inequality, especially in the employment sector. Undoubtedly Southeast Asia, as much as Asia, has achieved tremendous growth in economic terms in recent decades;[2] the region, however, contains economies at every stage of development, ranging from the poor to the rich. At the one end of the spectrum are countries like Cambodia and Timor-Leste where economic growth levels have been low; at the other, are countries like Singapore with a thriving economy that has propelled it into a developed nation. The economic boom in some countries clearly has had positive spillover effects on the ground on women. As in elsewhere in Asia, Southeast Asian women have reaped off the benefits of economic progress: many more women now, compared with the generations earlier, occupy high-level positions in the workplace (Brooks 2006); greater numbers of women than men are receiving a tertiary-level education; and, many more women at this time have increased their choices in their personal lives, whether to opt for a family life or become careerists (Stivens 2007).

Yet there remains scores of women who have been left behind in this path toward rapid economic growth. Impoverished and mostly from the rural areas, often these women have little education and skills and, therefore, are forced to take on low-paid and low-status jobs with little opportunity for upward social mobility. Since the mid-1960s when many countries in the region gradually adopted the export-oriented model of economic development, factory jobs were generated as a result, drawing mostly low-skilled women workers.

Capitalism thrived further under neo-liberalism principles in the 1980s, which resulted in the creation of more jobs. The removal of trade barriers, deregulation and privatization simultaneously promoted a climate for foreign direct investment to fuel economic growth. Multinational corporations capitalized on these environments by setting up manufacturing and production facilities in the developing countries and tapping on cheap labour. Following the earlier decades, the jobs afforded by these emerging sectors were mainly low-paid and low-end and, therefore, quickly absorbed women (Heyzer and Tan 1988; Bahramitash 2005). Thus, many women ended up in exploitative situations (Fatimah 1985; Lindio-McGovern 2007; Makin 2006). Describing women workers in the Export Processing Zones in Asia, a Hong Kong NGO reports the following (see Matsui 1999, p. 175):

The average age of women workers is from 16 to 25 years ... [and] their wages are low, around US$1 a day in Vietnam, China and Indonesia. They perform late-night work, and the ventilation and lighting are poor in their working environment ... Their domitories are crowded. They undergo sexual harassment and sexual violence both while commuting to work and on the work site. They are limited in the number of times they can take toilet breaks. Only single women are employed and those who marry must retire ... Most factories prohibit the organizing of trade unions. Nevertheless, workers have engaged in strikes and protest actions, pressing for wage increases and improved working conditions in the Philippines, Indonesia, Malaysia, China and Korea. Some workers have been arrested.

Evidently women entered the growing employment sectors as inferior labour; aside from being cheap, women workers were perceived to be docile and submissive — characteristics sought after by (male) employers. But it must be noted that women were not thrust into these jobs; many readily accepted these opportunities because wage work was an attractive option for these women who were mostly non-wage workers prior to entering the formal employment sector (Garcia-Dungo 2007).

The expansion of global markets also stirred migration. Many women migrated from the rural to urban areas in search of jobs while others traversed national borders to enter these work sectors, only to find that their rights are violated because often the working conditions are poor and wages are low.

The growth of multinational corporations has also led to women's engagement in home-bound work with little if not no security benefits (Mehrotra and Biggeri 2002). But women take on such work not only because of not having the appropriate skills to engage in more skilled work; there is the added complexity for cultural norms continue to dictate that women are the primary caregivers in the family, and so women take on jobs which allow them to work from home so that they can provide care to their children while engaging in wage work at the same time. Thus, although the last twenty years has seen "women's overall economic activity rates increased ... yet women's status in the labour market remains significantly inferior to that of men's...." (United Nations Millennium Project (UNMP) Report, as cited in Jones 2005), in part because development tended to be profit-focused, while ignoring its implications on gender.

Neo-liberalism accompanied by economic restructuring of various forms has also significant consequences on women's lives in other ways. For example, liberalization and structural adjustment coupled with cuts in social spending have created heavy debt repayments. The inability to pay back has been argued to be the cause of women's declining health in the poorer countries of the developing south (Jagger 2002).

Furthermore, overt and covert manifestations of patriarchy continue to be prevalent in spite of the practice of bilateralism in the local culture of the region (Mazidah and Nik 1986; Ong 1987). In recent times, the region has seen the emergence of fundamentalisms, particularly religious fundamentalisms. Conservative Islamic classes have been demanding female purity through the veiling of women in certain countries. A disjuncture, however, arises between the insider perspective on the meanings attached to wearing the headscarf (Nagata 1995) and the interpretation of scholars, mainly feminists, who have argued that veiling places restrictions on women's dress codes and by extension is deemed a cultural practice reinscribing the subordination of women. Yet it must be remembered that the current trend of increasing Islamization cannot be divorced from state politics with women's bodies as the site for contestation. In this case, "gender politics are seldom merely about gender", as Ong (1995, p. 187) notes, but rather "they represent and crystallize nationwide struggles over a crisis of cultural identity, development, class formation, and the changing kinds of imagined community that are envisioned". In this milieu, it is of no surprise then that concerns over women's behaviour and movements have brought forth a host of Muslim women's groups and activists working toward achieving women's rights and justice (Norani 2005).

For many women, thus, by virtue of their gender identity, one disadvantage has the potential of translating into a myriad of other disadvantages: as girls, they are more likely to receive less education than boys and, therefore, face greater problems gaining employment in adulthood; as adults, they are prone to various reproductive health risks much earlier than men which are compounded should they be from the rural areas because of the difficulties in accessing proper healthcare services; women also face greater obstacles in entering some spheres in the public domain such as politics because of the lack of social networks and unfair practices that exclude them, and encounter discrimination by religions that reinscribe gender inequality through their teachings.

The gender gap, thus, continues to be pervasive in many domains. The gap varies, however, depending largely on context. Because economic development and the distribution of the benefits of growth have been uneven across the region as well as within countries, Southeast Asian women's experiences, interests, and concerns differ across the region, as in many other parts of the world. The chapters in this volume provide an insight into and analysis of the broad trends — including changes and continuities — in the experiences, interests and concerns of Southeast Asian women. These trends related to women are examined in the following arenas — the family, economic participation, politics, health, and religion. In some arenas, the trends are indicative of the kinds of disadvantages women face, which in turn have led to gender gaps; in other areas, women's progress has been found to eclipse men's, although this tends to be the exception by and large.

In chapter 2, Gavin W. Jones examines the changes in women's role in the family, in the face of dramatic contextual changes — globalization, economic growth, urbanization, educational development, and increasing levels of workforce participation of women in urban areas. He concludes that these variables have had major effects on marriage — whether to marry, when to marry, whether child-raising can be combined with the demands of the workforce, and intra-family power structures. Clearly a gender gap continues to persist in many areas in Southeast Asian women's lives. In the context of the family, cultural norms continue to assert women's role as primary caregiver. The problems related to having to balance the caregiver and worker roles have implications on married women's ability to advance in the workplace. This has impacts on decisions for family size. But the shrinking fertility across Southeast Asia is also a result of increasing non-marriage, especially in the more developed economies in the region.

That economic development across the region has been uneven has led to increasing population mobility within countries and across national boundaries. The demand for women workers in certain labour sectors has brought on what is called the feminization of migration. Bernadette P. Resurreccion's contribution in chapter 3 outlines how migration has become an important avenue for seeking employment driven by the process of globalization in which flows of people — increasingly women — move from rural to urban areas, from one region to the next, and across national borders. While large numbers of women migrate for work, this is a trend that is distinct from the past when mainly men took on employment abroad. The migration of women, however, has reproduced gender stereotypes by way of the kinds of jobs women take on. The kind of employment women take on reflects gender, she maintains, as the kind of work women migrants engage in is closely associated with reproductive and care work. But migrating for work for many of these women has problems. Women's work, as Resurreccion argues, is increasingly flexible, unregulated and unprotected, insecure, and dispensable with usually no employment benefits because the work they take on falls between informal and formal employment. Because women's work falls within that fine line between the formal and informal sectors, she contends for the re-definition of the notion of 'worker', departing from the conventional notion of formal employment.

A gender gap is also evident in the literature analysis of politics in Southeast Asia as a result of very few scholars asking questions related to gender. The extent to which authors have paid little attention to women's role in Southeast Asian politics is the focus of the fourth chapter by Susan Blackburn. While women clearly have lower political participation rates than men, they appear to be discriminated further when political scientists pay little attention to women's role in the domain. The chapter more specifically examines why some political scientists do better than others in recognizing the relevance of studying women's engagement in politics, and what this tells us about political science as a discipline. Blackburn adds that while some questions posed by political scientists are potentially fruitful as far as the study of gender is concerned (for example, questions about civil society and the democratization process), other areas of enquiry, such as the causes of regime change, and political economy and international relations, are sorely neglected.

In the area of women's health, progress towards mainstreaming gender has been slow or even impeded. In chapter 5, Rashidah Shuib contends that primarily governments in the region are yet to take into cognizance the ideological framework of gender equality and are even conflicted in integrating a gender dimension into health policies and programmes because it would mean pushing for sexual and reproductive health and rights which are highly contentious issues. The author's argument is that in order for gender mainstreaming in health policies to take place, there has to be an ideological shift among policy-makers and a political will to see the importance of incorporating health rights into account. But prospects for a change in mindset and political commitment on the part of governments are dim because of specific social ideologies and the rise of religious fundamentalisms which act as obstacles to gender mainstreaming.

The arena of religion is also marked by discouraging prospects for women because of conservative interpretations of the holy texts. In chapter 6, Maznah Mohamad focuses on some controversial developments with regard to the issuance of new regulations, laws and religious opinions (*fatwa*) and their consequences on women. The rise of conservative Islamic forces in Southeast Asia is revealing in the contexts of dress code, conversion and marriage where only women's behaviour and appearance have become delimited and rigorously defined especially in Indonesia and Malaysia. While religion has been seen to place limits increasingly on women's movements through a number of legislations in these contexts, on the upside these legislations have spurred civil society engagement. However, the debates and dialogues have found little success in either changing the legislations or stopping the promulgation/implementation of these laws and policies, thereby indicating that women's freedom as individuals to direct their own mobility has become restricted.

Notes

1. For an historical account of women's integral role in economic and agricultural activities, see Andaya (2006) and Reid (1988).
2. In Asia, developing economies grew by 7.6 per cent in 2008 and are expected to grow by 7.8 per cent in 2009, although the percentage growth was 8.7 per cent, the highest in 19 years, in 2007. See Frank Harrigan, William James, Juthathip Jongwanich, and Lea Sumulong, "Asian Development Outlook: Part 1: The Global Slowdown and Developing Asia" <http://www.adb.org/Documents/Books/ADO/2008/part0101.asp> (accessed 8 January 2008).

References

Alexander, J. and P. Alexander. "Markets as Gendered Domain: The Javanese *Pasar*". In *Women Traders in Cross-Cultural Perspective: Mediating Identities, Marketing Wares*, edited by Linda J. Seligmann. Stanford, California: Stanford University Press, 2001.

Andaya, Barbara W. *The Flaming Womb: Repositioning Women in Early Modern Southeast Asia*. Honolulu: University of Hawaii Press, 2006.

Atkinson, Jane M. and Shelly Errington. *Power and Difference: Gender in Island Southeast*. Stanford, California: Stanford University Press, 1990.

Bahramitash, Roksana. *Liberation from Liberalization: Gender and Globalization in Southeast Asia*. London: Zed Books, 2005.

Brooks, Ann. *Gendered Work in Asian Cities: The New Economy and Changing Labour Markets*. England: Ashgate, 2006.

Dube, Leela. *Women and Kinship: Comparative Perspectives on Gender in South and South-East Asia*. Tokyo: United Nations University Press, 1997.

Fatimah Daud. *"Minah Karan": The Truth about Malaysian Factory Girls*. Kuala Lumpur: Berita Publishing, 1985.

Ford, Michele. "Responses to Changing Labour Relations: The Case of Women's NGOs in Indonesia". In *Women and Work in Globalising Asia*, edited by D-S. S. Gills and N. Piper. London: Routledge, 2002.

Garcia-Dungo, Nanette. *Negotiating from the Margin: Dynamics of Women's Work in a Globalized Agricultural Economy*. Diliman, Quezon City: The University of the Philippines Press, 2007.

Hay, M. Cameron. "Women Standing between Life and Death: Fate, Agency and the Healers of Lombok". *The Agency of Women in Asia*, edited by L. Parker. Singapore: Marshall Cavendish, 2005.

Harrigan, Frank, William James, Juthathip Jongwanich, and Lea Sumulong. "Asian Development Outlook: Part 1: The Global Slowdown and Developing Asia". <http://www.adb.org/Documents/Books/ADO/2008/part0101.asp> (accessed 8 January 2008).

Heyzer, Noeleen and Tan Boon Kean. "Work Skills and Consciousness of Women Workers in Asia". In *Daughters in Industry: Work Skills and Consciousness of Women Workers in Asia*, edited by Noeleen Heyzer. Kuala Lumpur: Asian and Pacific Development Centre, 1988.

Human Development Report 2006. "The State of Human Development". United Nations Development Programme <http://hdr.undp.org/en/media/thestateofh umandevelopment.pdf> (accessed 5 January 2009).

Hutheesing, M.O.L. Klein. "Study Approaches to Gender in Malaysia". *The Indian Journal of Social Sciences* 7, nos. 3 and 4 (1994): 341–54.

Jagger, A.M. "Vulnerable Women and Neo-liberal Globalization: Debt Burdens Undermine Women's Health in the Global South". *Theoretical Medicine* 23 (2002): 425–40.

Jamilah Ariffin. *Women and Development in Malaysia*. Petaling Jaya: Pelanduk Publications, 1992.

Li, Tania. *Malays in Singapore: Culture, Economy and Ideology*. New York and Singapore: Oxford University Press, 1989.

Lindio-McGovern, L. "Neo-liberal Globalization in the Philippines: Its Impact on Filipino Women and their Forms of Resistance". *Journal of Developing Societies* 23, nos. 1–2 (2007): 15–35.

Makin, Jennifer. "Cambodia: Women and Work in the Garment Industry". Report by ILO Better Factories Cambodia and World Bank Justice for the Poor Program. Phnom Penh, Cambodia, 2006.

Matsui, Yayori. *Women in the New Asia: From Pain to Power*. London: Zed Books, 1999.

Mazidah Zakaria and Nik Safiah Karim. "Women in Development: The Case of an All-Women Youth Land Development Scheme in Malaysia". In *Visibility and Power: Essays on Women in Society and Development*, edited by L. Dube, E. Leacock, and S. Ardener. Delhi: Oxford University Press, 1986.

Medina, Belen T.G. *The Filipino Family*, 2nd ed. Diliman, Quezon City: University of the Philippines Press, 2001.

Mehrotra, Santosh and Mario Biggeri. "Social Protection in the Informal Economy: Home Based Women Workers and Outsourced Manufacturing in Asia". Innocenti Working Papers, no. 97. Florence, Italy: United Nations Children's Fund, 2002.

Nagata, Judith. "Modern Malay Women and the Message of the 'Veil'". In *'Male' and 'Female' in Developing Southeast Asia*, edited by Wazir Jahan Karim. Oxford: Berg Publishers, 1995.

Ng, Cecilia, Maznah Mohamad, and tan beng hui. *Feminism and the Women's Movement in Malaysia: An Unsung (R)evolution.* New York: Routledge, 2006.

Norani Othman, ed. *Muslim Women and the Challenges of Islamic Extremism.* Petaling Jaya, Selangor: Sisters in Islam, 2005.

Ong, Aihwa. *Spirits of Resistance and Capitalist Discipline.* New York: State University of New York Press, 1987.

————. "State versus Islam: Malay Families, Women's Bodies, and the Body Politic in Malaysia". In *Bewitching Women, Pious Men: Gender and Body Politics in Southeast Asia,* edited by Aihwa Ong and Michael G. Peletz. Berkeley: University of California Press, 1995.

Reid, A. "Female Roles in Pre-colonial Southeast Asia". *Modern Asian Studies* 22, no. 3 (1988): 629–45.

Stivens, Maila. *Matiliny and Modernity: Sexual Politics and Social Change in Rural Malaysia.* Australia: Allen and Unwin, 1996.

————. "Post-modern Motherhoods and Cultural Contest in Malaysia and Singapore". In *Working and Mothering in Asia: Images, Ideologies and Identities,* edited by T.W. Devasahayam and B.S.A. Yeoh. Singapore and Copenhagen: National University of Singapore Press and Nordic Institute of Asian Studies Press, 2007.

Stoler, A. "Class Structure, Female Autonomy in Rural Java". *Signs* 3, no. 1 (1977): 74–89.

Strange, Heather. *Rural Women in Tradition and Transition.* New York: Praeger, 1981.

Sullivan, Norma M. *Masters and Managers: A Study of Gender Relations in Urban Java.* Sydney: Allen and Unwin, 1994.

"The Global Gender Gap Report 2008: Country Highlights and Profiles" <http://www.weforum.org/en/initiatives/gcp/Gender%20Gap/Countries2008/index.htm> (accessed 4 January 2009).

United Nations Millennium Project (UNMP) Report 2005. Taskforce on Education and Gender Equality. *Taking Action: Achieving Gender Equality and Empowering Women* <http://unmp.forumone.com/eng_html_02.html> (accessed January 2005) as cited in Rochelle Jones, "Shape up or ship out: Why Millennium Goal No. 3 can not be achieved until the multilateral institutions stop imposing neo-liberal policy on the rest of the world", 2005 <http://www.globalizacija.com/doc_en/e0019neo.htm> (accessed 5 January 2009).

Wazir Jahan Karim. *Women and Culture: Between Malay Adat and Islam.* Boulder: Westview, 1992.

————, ed. *'Male' and 'Female' in Developing Southeast Asia.* Oxford: Berg Publishers, 1995.

Zohra A. Baso and Nurul Ilmi Idrus. "Women's Activism against Violence in South Suluwesi". In *Women in Indonesia: Gender, Equity and Development,* edited by K. Robinson and S. Bessell. Singapore: Institute of Southeast Asian Studies, 2002.

2

WOMEN, MARRIAGE AND FAMILY IN SOUTHEAST ASIA

Gavin W. Jones

INTRODUCTION

The main aim of this chapter is to look at changes in women's role in the family, in the face of dramatic contextual changes — globalization, economic growth, urbanization, educational development, and the increasing levels of workforce participation of women in urban areas. These have major effects on marriage — whether to marry, when to marry, whether child-raising can be combined with the demands of the workforce, and intra-family power structures.

The last half century has seen remarkable educational changes, from a situation of severe disadvantage for daughters in educational opportunity to one of near equality of opportunity, and indeed a female majority in tertiary education in a number of countries. What is remarkable is how universal these changes have been; what needs to be recognized is that they both contribute to, and are reflections of, changing attitudes to female roles.

More or less universally, the rising levels of education have made for increasing levels of female participation in the urban workforce. Although equality in incomes for equal work has not been achieved, the situation is much improved, and the excess of women in higher education means that many higher-status jobs are now going to women. Many women are also going abroad as migrant workers — more than two million Filipinas and one million Indonesians at any one time. Is this a reflection of broader opportunities opened up by education, or rather a reflection of the poor earning opportunities in the poorer countries of the region? It is no doubt both, but we should certainly keep in mind that even those going abroad as domestic servants from countries such as the Philippines and Indonesia typically have above average levels of education compared to others in their home areas.

A NOTE ON SOUTHEAST ASIAN FAMILY STRUCTURES

Before turning to the main theme of this chapter — the changing patterns of marriage and fertility in Southeast Asia and what they tell us about women's family roles — a general note on the Southeast Asian family may be in order. Southeast Asia is differentiated from the kinship system dominated by Confucianist traditions that characterizes much of East Asia, and the joint family of the Indian subcontinent, by its bilateral kinship system, which provides for much more flexibility in post-marital residence. The Minangkabau and Acehnese follow matrilineal patterns, and even in Thailand, matrilineal ties are the most important. Men normally move into their wife's parents' household for a period of one to three years and then establish a separate, economically independent household. This pattern is also the traditional one among the Malays in Malaysia, in Indonesia and in the Philippines (Medina 2001). The positive aspects of such kinship systems for women's status are hinted at by the fact that no Southeast Asian country other than Vietnam has experienced unusually high sex ratios at birth due to misuse of prenatal diagnostic techniques for non-medical purposes, which in both China and India has resulted in the practice of foeticide on a very large scale as a result of strong son preference (Attane and Guilmoto, eds. 2007). Vietnam is the one country of Southeast Asia that does not follow a bilateral kinship system, and its problems with misuse of ultrasound techniques (Nhan and Mai 2008) put it more in the Chinese than in the Southeast Asian camp in this regard.

The distinction between family and household needs to be kept in mind. Family links remain strong to the level of cousins and often second cousins. In countries such as Indonesia, children are frequently "lent" to relatives who are childless or otherwise well placed to raise them. But the household — those who actually live together — is growing smaller, as a result of lower fertility, and the movement of many young people from rural areas to the cities. It is important to keep in mind that households may have alternating periods of being nuclear and joint. This is because of flexibility about who lives with whom in the bilateral kinship systems that characterize the region and also the changing structure of the family as children grow up, grandparents die, and other changes occur.

WOMEN'S EDUCATION AND EMPLOYMENT

The trends in education and employment lie at the heart of women's changing roles in the family and society, and require a brief summary. The broad trends in education are shown in Figures 2.1 and 2.2. They demonstrate a revolution in gender balance in educational opportunities, and indeed a situation has arisen in many countries of the region where the majority of tertiary students are females (although this is not the case at the postgraduate level). This being acknowledged, it is too early to say that discrimination towards girls in education has ended or that they face no problems in continuing their

FIGURE 2.1

Ratio of per cent of females to per cent of males who have had at least lower secondary education, by age group, 1990 or later years

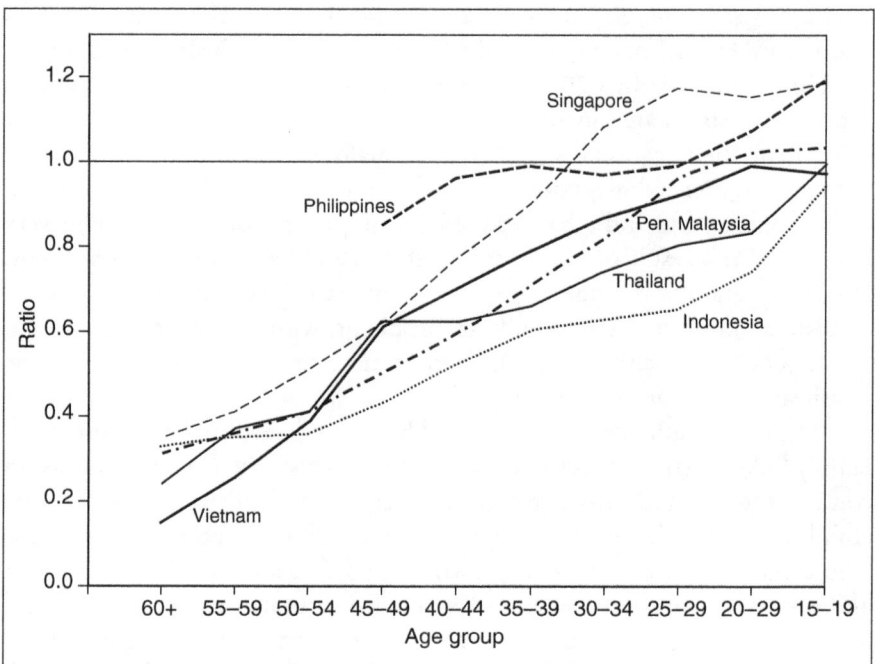

Source: Knodel and Jones (1996).

FIGURE 2.2

Ratio of Sex-Specific Enrolment Rates in Malaysia, 1970–2003

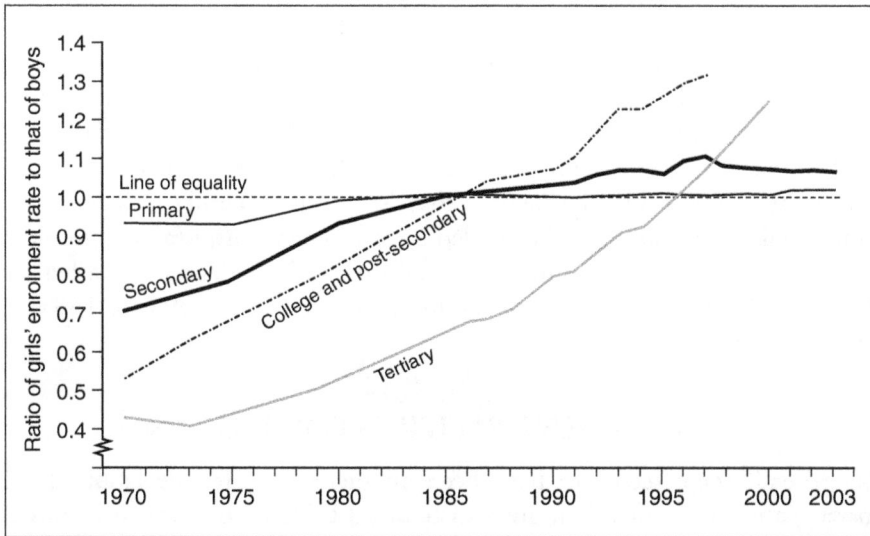

Source: Leete (2007), Figure 7.1.

education (on Indonesia, see Oey-Gardiner 1997, pp. 145–52). What is found in many rural areas of Indonesia, for example, is that although a small number of parents still favour educating sons over daughters for traditional reasons, the reason why many parents are loath to continue sending their daughters to school is that the school is distant and this exposes the girl to dangers along the way (Oey-Gardiner 1991), or that schools lack even basic toilet and washroom facilities, requiring defecation or urination in streams, fishponds or nearby fields (Warta CIMU 2002, p. 12).

Nevertheless, the situation in which young unmarried women and men are mixing freely in tertiary educational institutions, at ages at which most of these young women would traditionally have long been married, symbolizes the basic changes in the familial and social setting which young people now face. Not only this, but more or less universally, rising levels of female education, along with increasing urbanization, have made for rising levels of female participation in the kinds of work that takes them outside the household. This means a considerable loosening of traditional restrictions on the social contacts of unmarried, as well as married, women.

All this has affected intra-family power structures. For one thing, the superior performance of girls in school, documented widely through the region and, indeed, beyond, seems to reflect problems for males in finding appropriate role models. Their role models are further challenged by the post-schooling trajectories of girls in the household. In cultures in which males are supposed to be the earning members of the household, and in which fathers and brothers are supposed to exercise control over the behaviour of daughters and sisters, male self-esteem is threatened by finding that it is the daughter (sister) who is earning the income that is crucial to family well-being. In some Malaysian examples, this has led to considerable intra-familial tension, with young women increasingly asserting their independence and fathers or brothers resisting change in the traditional order (Jones 1994, p. 148 and references cited therein).

EMPLOYMENT PATTERNS FOR WOMEN

In general, there seems to have been an increase in female labour force participation rates in urban areas of Southeast Asian countries over recent decades. I say "urban" advisedly because measurement of female labour force participation in rural areas is difficult, and measurement of trends even more difficult, because surveys used to show change may be measuring different things. Thus measured female labour force participation in Thailand has always been very high, partly, it seems, because farmers' wives have automatically been classified as working in Thai censuses and surveys. This is a sensible procedure, I think, but it is not followed in other countries, which tend to show lower levels of female workforce participation in rural areas. Community and voluntary work is another part of the life of many women that goes under-recorded (and this contributes to its under-valuation) in conventional data on the labour force.

Horton (1999) concluded, based on analysis of available labour force surveys (from the 1960s to the 1990s) from Asia, Latin America, North Africa and the Middle East, that women's labour force participation is tending to increase over time, along with a shift out of agriculture into other industries and occupations. This conclusion seems to hold for some countries of Southeast Asia — certainly, for Singapore, Malaysia, Philippines and Indonesia (Manning 1998, Table 9.1). But for others the evidence is less clear. The more important point to make — and the evidence here *is* clear — is that there has been a very substantial shift out of agricultural activities into secondary and tertiary sector employment, much of it of course in urban areas, but some of it reflecting increasing non-agricultural employment in areas classified as rural.

The other point to emphasize is that trends in education have directly influenced women's labour force participation. The decision by girls — and their parents — to continue to higher levels of education is, after all, largely directed towards finding suitable employment. Therefore it is hardly surprising that female labour force participation rates tend to be highest among women with tertiary education. Frequently it is found that it is the least educated and the best educated women who are most likely to be in the labour force — to put it crudely, the former by dint of necessity and the latter by dint of opportunity. Completion of secondary education and, even more, getting a tertiary degree, opens up a wide range of employment opportunities for women, and so the percentage who work among these educational attainment groups tends to be high.

DELAYED MARRIAGE AND NON-MARRIAGE

The factors above are highly relevant to understanding trends in marriage in the region. The trends in marriage in this previously "universal marriage" region are quite marked — towards later and less marriage (see Table 2.1). Thailand, Myanmar, Malaysia and Singapore show the most marked delays in marriage, but the trend is universal throughout the region, except in Vietnam. The Philippines already had a relatively late marriage pattern in 1960, and has not shown much increase since then. The trends towards later marriage are most pronounced in the cities of the region, and among better educated women (Jones 2005).

The available evidence from Southeast Asia from 1980, 1990 and 2000 population censuses shows a marked gradation in proportions of women never married by educational level, controlling for age. Those with tertiary education had by far the highest proportions of never-married (see Figure 2.3). This was the case, for example, for Peninsular Malaysia, Thailand, Myanmar, and the Philippines, and for the major metropolises of Bangkok, Singapore and Jakarta (Quah 1990, 1998; Xenos and Gultiano 1992, p. 22; Guest and Tan 1994; Jones 1997, pp. 58–60; Jones 2004, pp. 10–14). Data for two smaller cities in Indonesia (Medan and Yogyakarta) also confirm the relation-ship (Situmorang 2007, Table 5).

Tables 2.2, 2.3 and 2.4 provide more recent data showing the strong association of proportions remaining single and advanced levels of education, and the inverse association in the case of men. While there is no space in this chapter to deal in detail with marriage issues facing males, it should be noted that in many countries of the region, there is evidence that it is the more poorly educated males who are less likely to marry, presumably both because their economic situation discourages them from marrying and starting a family, and also because they occupy a very low status in the marriage market.

FIGURE 2.3

Percentage of Females Never Married by Age and Education, Singapore, 2005 and Thailand, 2000

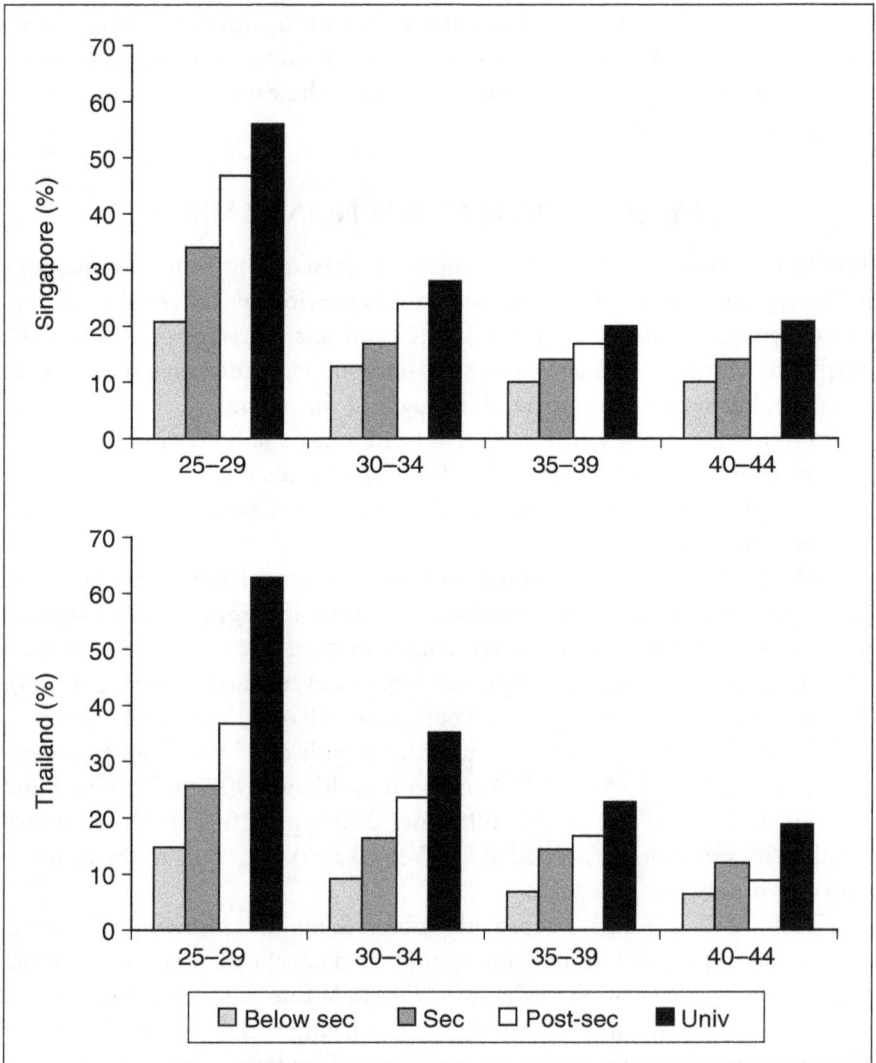

Source: Singapore data calculated from *General Household Survey 2005* and the Thailand data from the 2000 Population Census of Thailand.

TABLE 2.1
Indicators of Trends in Age at Marriage for Females, Various Southeast Asian Countries, 1960–2005

Country	1960	1970	1980	1990	2000	2005
Singulate mean age at marriage						
Cambodia	21.3	n.a.	n.a.	n.a.	22.5	22.8
Indonesia	n.a.	19.3	20.0	21.6	22.7	23.4
Malaysia	20.3	22.1	23.5	24.6	24.9	n.a.
Myanmar	n.a.	21.3	22.4	24.5	25.8	n.a.
Philippines	n.a.	22.8	22.4	23.8	n.a.	n.a.
Singapore	n.a.	24.2	26.2	27.0	26.5	26.9
Thailand	22.4	22.0	22.8	23.5	24.1	n.a.
Vietnam	n.a.	n.a.	n.a.	23.0	22.8	23.1
Percentage never married, age 30–34						
Cambodia	4.2	n.a.	n.a.	n.a.	10.0	9.5
Indonesia	n.a.	2.2	3.4	4.5	6.9	8.1
Malaysia	2.6	5.7	9.9	12.1	12.1	n.a.
Myanmar	n.a.	9.3	12.8	19.6	25.9	n.a.
Philippines	11.6	11.7	11.9	13.4	14.8	n.a.
Singapore	n.a.	9.6	16.7	20.9	19.5	22.1
Thailand	6.7	8.1	11.8	14.1	16.1	n.a.
Vietnam	n.a.	n.a.	n.a.	10.9	9.8	9.4

Source: Jones (2005), Table 1; Jones and Gubhaju (2008).

TABLE 2.2
Proportion Never Married by Age, Sex and Educational Level, Singapore, 2000 and 2005

	Below secondary		Secondary		Post-secondary		University	
	2000	2005	2000	2005	2000	2005	2000	2005
Males								
25–29	62	67	58	63	70	69	69	73
30–34	40	42	29	35	28	33	28	32
35–39	28	29	18	22	15	18	13	14
40–44	21	23	14	14	9	12	7	8
Females								
25–29	21	21	30	34	43	47	54	56
30–34	13	13	17	17	23	24	27	28
35–39	10	10	14	14	20	17	23	20
40–44	9	10	15	14	20	18	22	21

Source: Yap (2008), Table 8.3.

TABLE 2.3
Percentage Never Married by Age and Education, Thailand, 2000

Sex and age	Completed primary or less	Lower secondary	Upper secondary	Tertiary	All levels
Females					
25–29	14.8	25.5	36.7	62.9	29.1
30–34	9.3	16.4	23.8	35.1	15.6
35–39	7.0	14.3	17.0	22.7	10.7
40–44	6.3	11.9	8.7	18.9	8.5
45–49	5.9	12.2	11.8	17.5	7.4
Males					
25–29	36.7	42.0	48.0	67.1	45.0
30–34	17.2	21.1	22.7	34.4	21.3
35–39	9.4	13.2	14.3	18.7	11.8
40–44	6.1	6.8	9.4	9.2	6.8
45–49	3.9	6.2	5.8	7.3	4.6

Source: Unpublished data from the 2000 population census.

TABLE 2.4
Percentage Never Married by Age and Education, Bangkok, 2000

	Primary or less	Lower secondary	Upper secondary	Tertiary	All levels
Females					
25–29	25.0	30.2	41.6	73.5	50.9
30–34	17.7	21.4	28.2	48.9	31.8
35-39	14.8	18.9	23.7	36.2	23.8
40–44	13.3	16.2	21.8	29.8	19.2
45–49	12.7	17.2	20.4	24.7	16.5
Males					
25–29	37.7	46.6	52.6	78.1	58.9
30–34	23.3	28.3	32.3	48.8	35.3
35–39	16.5	20.4	20.9	29.3	22.4
40–44	12.1	13.7	15.6	17.8	14.6
45–49	9.1	11.7	13.5	12.4	11.0

Source: Unpublished data from the 2000 population census.

REASONS AND MOTIVATION FOR
DELAYED MARRIAGE

The effect of education and changing patterns of labour force participation are central to these marriage changes. In Indonesia, the proportion of young women aged 15–19 and 20–24 who are either in school or working in the formal sector has risen steadily over the last three decades (Hull 2003, Table 3). This reflects a changing life course trajectory for young women, in which marriage is postponed and young women do not simply follow their parents' choice in the matter. Traditionally in Southeast Asia, women needed a husband for the economic security he afforded, and to fulfill traditional expectations, which made marriage mandatory for any woman who was not physically or mentally handicapped. But with changing education and work patterns, a large cohort of women was created who not only had an independent income but for whom marriage and its expected outcome — childbearing — would cause tangible disadvantages in disruption to their career and loss of independence.

The factors making for delayed marriage in the region are complex, but can perhaps be divided into three categories.

Perceived Desirability of Marriage

Among the most important factors in this category are:

- **Expansion of education:** In the poorer countries in the group, notably Indonesia, this meant that girls remain in school beyond the ages at which they traditionally married, but more importantly, educational expansion and trends in labour markets have opened up employment possibilities for women, widened their aspirations and freed many from financial dependence on men. "Later and less" marriage has particularly characterized the growing group of women with tertiary education.
- **Increasing uncertainty in the labour market, felt in varying degrees throughout the region:** As a result, men and couples in serious relationships, are reluctant to marry until they can build up some capital, and women are increasingly cautious about marrying a man with poor earnings prospects.
- **Rising divorce rates:** Rising divorce rates in many countries of the region are probably leading to increasing caution in choosing a marriage partner.
- **Increasing urbanization and work pressures:** The growing urban populations in countries such as Singapore, Malaysia, Thailand and

Indonesia face issues of work pressures, including very long hours of work (especially when travel to and from work is included), and housing affordability.

- **Changes in perception of sexuality:** These are also increasingly sexually permissive societies, meaning that access to sex outside of marriage is easier to come by.[1] The recent passage of the pornography law in Indonesia may seem to contradict this, but passage of this law can be seen to reflect the concern of many, particularly traditionalist Muslims, that permissiveness is getting out of hand.

Disincentives to Have Children

Marriage can rarely be separated from its expected outcome in Southeast Asia: that is, the bearing and raising of children. An important issue is the extent to which trends in non-marriage are behaviourally and motivationally linked to trends in fertility. To what extent do people avoid marriage because they want to avoid having children? It is likely that in Southeast Asia, where strong pressure is placed on those who marry to have a child quickly, the most straightforward way to avoid having children is not to marry (Jones 2004, p. 17). Therefore factors relating to reluctance to begin raising a family also work against marriage:

- The costs of childrearing are increasing, both the direct financial costs and the opportunity costs of women's interrupted career development.
- There is increasing pressure, especially in the cities, to engage in "intensive parenting", bringing children the benefits of coaching, music lessons, etc. and ensuring that the child is "successful". Women bear the brunt of fulfilling societal expectations about intensive parenting.
- In the face of only glacial change in men's attitudes towards their role in household management and childcare, women who can expect to be economically independent are aware of the difficulty of finding a mate who shares their values and expectations, and increasingly uncertain about the value to place on marriage and family formation.

Marriage Squeeze

The decline in arranged marriage has cast the onus of finding a spouse onto the individuals concerned, but a well-developed marriage market has not emerged (although there are interesting developments in commercial and Internet matchmaking; see Jones and Gubhaju 2008).

The trends in education and employment already discussed provide an entirely new context for marriage markets. Whereas the traditional emphasis on hypergamy — women marrying up — made sense when educated women were an aberration and were greatly outnumbered by educated men, it becomes impossible to sustain when women become the majority of educated persons in the marriageable ages.

A brief description of the issue of "marriage squeeze" for educated women in Southeast Asian cities is perhaps needed. The first point is that the almost universal decline in fertility throughout the region has until recently not altered the shape of the population pyramid at the marriageable ages, in which successively larger cohorts have been moving up the pyramid. Given the traditional gap in marriage ages for males and females, this makes for an excess of marriageable females. This is particularly so in some metropolitan cities of the region, where sex ratios are lowered by female-dominated migration patterns: the sex ratio among recent migrants aged 15–24 in 2000 was 60 males per 100 females in Metro Manila, 62 in Jakarta and 84 in Bangkok; at ages 25–34 it was 91 in Metro Manila, 95 in Bangkok but 123 in Jakarta (Jones and Douglass, eds. 2008, chapter 11). Equally important in recent decades, the great improvements in educational opportunities in Southeast Asian countries have been even more marked for females than for males, as already discussed. This has lowered the ratio of well-educated men to well-educated women in marriageable age cohorts. Further, educated women have been delaying marriage to establish themselves in their career. Given the persistence of traditional norms about suitable marriage partners, which favour choice by men of brides who are younger and less educated than themselves, once educated women reach the point of looking seriously for a spouse, they are likely to find slim pickings in the field of potential mates. The problem is exacerbated by a "values gap" between educated women and many of their potential spouses. Feminist values have been increasingly adopted by educated women in the region, but male attitudes towards gender roles, including sharing of housework and the raising of children have been slower to change (Quah 1998, chapter 5). Thus many educated women in the region would share the perception, and experience, that the problem of the marriage market is not so much the lack of available males as the shortage of men who share their values and expectations (Hull 2002, p. 8).

Let us take one example — Malaysia. Assume that the average age gap between husbands and wives is five years — as indeed it used to be in Malaysia, then we can compare the numbers of men aged 20–49 with secondary education or more with the number of women 15–45 with the same level of education. In 1970, the ratio of these numbers was 1.17. In 1980 it was 0.99, in 1990 1.01, and by 2000 0.82. In other words, the 1990s saw a change from a situation where numbers of males and females in these age-education groups were approximately equal at the beginning of the decade to one where there were 22 per cent more females than males at the end of the decade. In light of these figures, increasing non-marriage for educated women is not hard to understand.

SINGLEHOOD AND ITS DISCONTENTS

Stein (1981) argued that the state of being single can be categorized based on an element of choice (voluntary versus involuntary) and permanence (temporary and stable), and that membership in these categories changes over time and with changing situations. Survey information in Singapore showing a general desire to marry (Quah 1998; Chan 2002) suggests that there is a good deal of involuntary singlehood around, and this is probably the case more widely in Southeast Asia.

With the rise of singlehood throughout the region, the key question is: "what is the role of single men and women in the family?" The fact of increased singlehood does not mean that these single people, particularly single women, do not play key roles in their families. One point to bear in mind is that compared with Western countries, single young women are far more likely to be still living with their parents. They are still linked into familial networks of care and concern. Indeed, in Myanmar, one reason for women to remain single — a reason validated by community attitudes — is to care for their parents in old age.

But it is also the case that institutions are slow to change, and the cohorts of women who are "pioneers" in delaying their marriage have to face the brunt of the disconnect between reality and societal expectations. Thus, it would be naive to think that women remaining single in their late twenties and thirties do not face problems. A study in Indonesia (Situmorang 2007) highlighted some of these, including pressures to marry, social stigma because of their single status, and programmes and policies including reproductive and sexual health that are restricted to the married and, therefore, discriminate against the growing number of never married. All women interviewed in this study agreed that life would be easier for them if people, including families and friends, would treat the never married as a 'normal' person.

DECLINING FERTILITY

A major factor related to the changing role of women in the workforce is the decline in fertility rates experienced in Southeast Asian countries. Delayed marriage is partly responsible, but even within marriage, childbearing is becoming less common. Low fertility (approximately replacement level or even below) is now characteristic of: ethnic Chinese and Indians (Singapore, Malaysia), Thailand, Myanmar, Vietnam, and most of Indonesia. Higher fertility is characteristic of: Malays (although coming down, and at replacement level among Malay Singaporeans), some provinces of Indonesia, Philippines, Cambodia (although coming down), and Lao PDR.

There are substantial urban-rural differences in fertility levels. Fertility tends to be lowest in the major metropolitan areas, such as Singapore, Bangkok, Jakarta and Kuala Lumpur. In Manila, fertility is also lower than elsewhere in the country, though even in Manila, it remains above replacement level, reflecting the overall maintenance of relatively high levels of fertility in the Philippines. Everywhere in Southeast Asia (as indeed throughout most of the world), educational differences in fertility levels can be observed, with an inverse relationship between a woman's level of education and her fertility.

The declines in fertility in Southeast Asia cannot match those in East Asian countries. Only Singapore can compare. Yet if we examine the fertility of certain sub-groups, we can see the prospect of very low levels of fertility being reached. At the national level, it has been argued that a total fertility rate sustained at levels of less than 1.5 has serious implications for future age structure and eventual population decline. In the region, Singapore, Bangkok and vicinity already have total fertility rates (TFRs) below this level, while Chinese Malaysians, Thailand as a whole and some provinces of Indonesia and states of Myanmar have TFRs of well below replacement level. The explanation of fertility trends in the region can only be partly explained through a traditional (development leads to lower fertility) model. This kind of model would fail to apply in Myanmar, and it would also fail to explain why the Malays in Malaysia, with much higher income and average educational levels than in Indonesia, until recently had a fertility rate one child higher than in Indonesia.

"WORK-LIFE BALANCE" ISSUES RELATED TO FERTILITY

I use the term "work-life balance", a term with the curious implication that work has nothing to do with life, only because it has such widespread currency. Anyway, there are many issues tied up with balancing the demands of the workplace and those of other aspects of people's lives in the "new" Southeast Asian family. Dual-income households are now much more common throughout the region.[2] But roles played in the family have been slower to change. Even in dual-income couples, women are still expected to play the major role in housework and the raising of children. Care of the elderly or dependant also falls primarily on women. Thus women are facing the double bind of labour force demands and housework, both requiring intensive time inputs. How is this to be achieved? Hochschild and Machung (1989) described the emergence of the "super-mom syndrome" in the United States. The super-mom is a woman who has successfully embraced the multiple roles of career woman/ideal wife/model mom. "There is no trace of stress, no suggestion that the mother needs help from others. She isn't harassed. She's busy, and it's glamorous to be busy" (Hochschild and Machung 1989, p. 23). I have noticed that women's magazines in Malaysia (and probably in other Southeast Asian countries) like to highlight successful career women who successfully raise a family at the same time.[3] Of course, unlike in the United States, they may have the help of domestic servants from poorer neighbouring countries. Despite the positive imagery, the strain of managing the demand of the workplace and the family cannot be gainsaid, and the traditional roles of wife and mother are looking increasingly less attractive to many women, especially to the better educated. This is a major reason for the steady decline in fertility rates throughout the region.

One other aspect of women's evolving work patterns and their gendered effect within the family is the childcare practices adopted by women juggling the demand of work and childrearing. In most Southeast Asian countries, childcare facilities, either commercial or subsidised by government or the workplace, are underdeveloped, partly because of the belief that the family should deal with the needs of its members. This leads to a heavy reliance on grandparents for the childcare needs of working mothers. Either the grandparent(s) care for the child or children, or in the case of upper middle class families, they supervise domestic helpers in this role. In both cases, the main burden falls on the grandmother, and it is not certain that it is a role that they would necessarily choose if they felt they had the option (Teo et al. 2006, chapter 9).

FAMILY IMPACTS OF INCREASED INTERNATIONAL MOVEMENT

There are many aspects of international movement that impact on the Southeast Asian family. The first is the large flow of labour migrants circulating within the region and beyond. Large numbers of Filipinas and Indonesians are leaving their families to work abroad as domestic servants and in other occupations. Many of these women are single, and their movement abroad is a factor delaying their marriage. For example, maids working in Singapore are forbidden from marrying during their contract period. They are also immediately repatriated if found to be pregnant. Many of these women, though, are already married, and many leave children behind to be cared for by others in their absence. This has major implications for the roles of their husbands, mothers and other family members.

Marriage migration of Southeast Asian women to other countries is another growing trend. Actually, it has been going on for a considerable period, in the case of Filipinas in particular, but the new development is the targeting of Southeast Asian brides (especially from Vietnam) by men in wealthier countries of the region — Taiwan, South Korea, Japan and Singapore. There are major adjustment issues for these brides in their country of settlement, issues which have been touched on in a number of studies (see e.g. chapters in Piper and Roces, eds. 2003; Constable, ed. 2005; Kim, ed. 2008).

SOME QUALIFICATIONS

This chapter has concentrated on the more advanced countries of Southeast Asia. It has had relatively little to say about the poorer and least urbanized countries — Cambodia and Lao PDR, for example — or the poorer and least urbanized areas within countries such as the Philippines and Indonesia. In these regions, the trends toward later and less marriage and low fertility have not proceeded as far or as quickly. But the distinction cannot be drawn too sharply. The fact is that many poor rural populations in Indonesia have low fertility, and sometimes considerable delay in marriage. Even more striking, poverty-stricken Myanmar matches Singapore, the wealthiest country in the region, in delayed marriage and non-marriage.[4]

As noted earlier, in terms of the continued flight from marriage and decline of fertility to ultra-low levels, the countries of Southeast Asia, with the exception of Singapore, cannot compete with East Asian countries including Japan, Korea, Taiwan, and Hong Kong. Does this mean that as their levels of economic development rise, we can expect their marriage and fertility trends to mirror those already occurring in East Asia? To a large extent, yes. But Southeast Asia does not mirror the Confucianist, patriarchal family traditions of East Asia, which have much to do with the way marriage and fertility trends are playing out there. We should, therefore, expect some differences from the East Asian pattern to emerge in these Southeast Asian countries as their development proceeds.

Notes

1. Increasing sexual permissiveness has been documented for countries as widely different as Japan (Retherford and Ogawa 2006, pp. 19–20) and Thailand (Arunrat 2008, pp. 200–01).
2. In Singapore in 2000, 40.9 per cent of all married couples were dual earners compared to 40.2 per cent where only the husbands worked.
3. This appears to be true as well of women's magazines in other Southeast Asian countries, though to a lesser extent, because in Malaysia the adoration of the successful businesswoman-cum-mother aligns well with the Malaysian government's stance promoting both pronatalism and developmentalism (Stivens 2007).
4. Special factors that appear to operate in the Myanmar case include the reluctance of both men and women to marry and establish a family in uncertain economic and political circumstances, the general unacceptability of divorce as a way of escaping an unsatisfactory marriage, and the fact that singlehood is socially acceptable, particularly when the motive is to look after aged parents.

References

Arunrat Tangmunkongvorakul. "Sexual Health in Transition: Adolescent Lifestyles and Relationships in Contemporary Chiang Mai, Thailand". Unpublished Ph.D thesis. National Centre for Epidemiology and Population Health, Australian National University, Canberra, 2008.

Attane, Isabelle and Christophe Guilmoto Guilmoto, eds. *Watering the Neighbour's Garden: The Growing Demographic Female Deficit in Asia*. Paris: Committee for International Cooperation in National Research in Demography, 2007.

Chan, David. *Attitudes on Family: Survey on Social Attitudes of Singaporeans 2001*. Singapore: Ministry of Community Development, Youth and Sports, 2002. Available online at: <http://www.mcys.gov.sg/MCDSFiles/Resource%5CMater ials%5CAttitudes_on_Family.pdf> (accessed 9 January 2009).

Constable, Nicole, ed. *Cross-border Marriages: Gender and Mobility in Transnational Asia*. Philadelphia: University of Pennsylvania Press, 2005.

Guest, Philip and Joo Ean Tan. *Transformation of Marriage Patterns in Thailand*. Salaya: Institute for Population and Social Research, Mahidol University, 1994.

Hochschild, Arlie R. and Anne Machung. *The Second Shift: Working Parents and the Revolution at Home*. New York: Viking, 1989.

Horton, S. "Marginalization Revisited: Women's Market Work and Pay, and Economic Development". *World Development* 27, no. 3 (1999): 571–82.

Hull, Terence H. "The Marriage Revolution in Indonesia". Paper presented at the Annual Meeting of the Population Association of America, Atlanta, 2002.

————. "Demographic Perspectives on the Future of the Indonesian Family". *Journal of Population Research* 20, no. 1 (2003): 51–65.

Jones, Gavin W. *Marriage and Divorce in Islamic Southeast Asia*. Singapore: Oxford University Press, 1994.

————. "The Demise of Universal Marriage in East and South-East Asia". In *The Continuing Demographic Transition*, edited by G.W. Jones, R.M. Douglas, J.C. Caldwell, and R.M. D'Souza. Oxford: Clarendon Press, 1997.

————. "The Changing Indonesian household". In *Women in Indonesia: Gender, Equity and Development*, edited by K. Robinson and S. Bessell. Singapore: Institute of Southeast Asian Studies, 2002.

————. "The Flight from Marriage in East and Southeast Asia". *Journal of Comparative Family Studies* 36, no. 1 (2005): 93–119.

Jones, Gavin W. and Bina Gubhaju. "Emerging Trends in Marriage in the Low Fertility Countries of East and Southeast Asia". Paper presented at the International Conference on Low Fertility and Reproductive Health in East and Southeast Asia, Hotel Grand Palace, Tokyo, 12–14 November 2008.

Jones, Gavin W. and Mike Douglass, eds., *The Rise of Mega-Urban Regions in Pacific Asia — Urban Dynamics in a Global Era*. Singapore: National University of Singapore Press, 2008.

Kim, Doo-Sub, ed. *Cross-border Marriage: Process and Dynamics*. Seoul: Institute of Population and Aging Research, Hanyang University, 2008.

Knodel, J. and G.W. Jones. "Post-Cairo Population Policy: Does Promoting Girls' Schooling Miss the Mark?" *Population and Development Review* 22, no. 4 (1996): 683–702.

Leete, Richard. *Malaysia: From Kampung to Twin Towers: 50 Years of Economic and Social Development*. Kuala Lumpur: Oxford Fajar, 2007.

Manning, Chris. *Indonesian Labour in Transition: An East Asian Success Story?* Cambridge: Cambridge University Press, 1998.

Medina, Belen T.G. *The Filipino Family*, 2nd ed. Diliman, Quezon City: University of the Philippines Press, 2001.

Mitton, Roger. "Sex and the Single Vietnamese Girl". *Straits Times*, 20 May 2007, p. 32.

Nhan, Vu Quy and Le Thi Phuong Mai. "Low Fertility Achievement and New Challenges to the Vietnam's Population and Family Planning Program". Paper presented at the International Conference on Low Fertility and Reproductive Health in East and Southeast Asia organized by Nihon University Population Research Institute, Tokyo, 12–14 November 2008.

Oey-Gardiner, M. "Gender Differences in Schooling in Indonesia". *Bulletin of Indonesian Economic Studies* 27, no. 1 (1991): 57–79.

————. "Educational Developments, Achievements and Challenges". In *Indonesian Assessment: Population and Human Resources*, edited by G.W. Jones and T.H. Hull. Singapore: Institute of Southeast Asian Studies, 1997.

Piper, Nicola and Mina Roces, eds. *Wife or Worker? Asian Women and Migration*. New York: Rowman and Littlefield Publishers, 2003.

Quah, Stella R. *Family in Singapore: Sociological Perspective*, 2nd ed. Singapore: Times Academic Press, 1998.

──────. *Home and Kin: Families in Asia*. Singapore: Eastern Universities Press, 2003.

Retherford, R.D. and N. Ogawa. "Japan's Baby Bust: Causes, Implications and Policy Responses". In *The Baby Bust: Who Will Do the Work? Who Will Pay the Taxes?*, edited by Fred R. Harris. Lanham, Maryland: Rowman and Littlefield Publishers, 2006.

Stein, Peter J. *Single Life: Unmarried Adults in Social Context*. New York: St. Martins Press, 1981.

Stivens, M. "Post-modern Motherhoods and Cultural Contest in Malaysia and Singapore". In *Working and Mothering in Asia: Images, Ideologies and Identities*, edited by T.W. Devasahayam and B.S.A. Yeoh. Singapore and Copenhagen: National University of Singapore Press and Nordic Institute of Asian Studies Press, 2007.

Situmorang, Augustina. "Staying Single in a Married World: Never-Married Women in Yogyakarta and Medan". *Asian Population Studies* 3, no. 3 (2007): 287–304.

Teo, Peggy, Kalyani Mehta, Leng Leng Thang, and Angelique Chan. *Ageing in Singapore: Service Needs and the State*. London: Routledge, 2006.

Tey, N.P. "Trends in Delayed and Non-Marriage in Peninsular Malaysia". *Asian Population Studies* 3, no. 3 (2007): 243–62.

Warta CIMU. Special Issue: A study of the school improvement grant program and its impact. Jakarta: Central Independent Monitoring Unit of the Scholarships and Grants Program, 2002.

Xenos, P. and S.A. Gultiano. "Trends in female and male age at marriage and celibacy in Asia". Papers of the Program on Population no. 120, Honolulu: East-West Center, 1992.

3

GENDER TRENDS IN MIGRATION AND EMPLOYMENT IN SOUTHEAST ASIA

Bernadette P. Resurreccion

INTRODUCTION

Labour migration is generally nothing new in Southeast Asia. However in recent decades, changes in the contexts and causes of mobility are due to the enormously reduced importance of geographical distances in determining boundaries of labour markets. This is largely as a result of improved transport and communication technologies and the role of 'globalization' in promoting the decline of a number of barriers, including institutional ones, to the rapid movement of capital, labour and information.

Migration in Southeast Asia has become an important process of globalization in which flows of people — increasingly women — move from rural to urban areas, from one region to the next, and across national borders in the context of growing 'global cities', and new urban and peri-urbanizing spaces in response to rapid industrialization.

A number of factors explain the exponential growth in female labour migration: the growth of formal and informal economies in the services sector and tourism industry in the region has created job opportunities for women, in addition to employment in garment and textile industries across national borders. Southeast Asian migrant women usually originate from countries with a relatively high female labour force participation rate. Hardship, especially in the rural areas, induces these women to employ labour migration as a means to survive. Additionally, there are relatively few cultural constraints in Southeast Asia that might constrain the mobility of women and, social networks have greatly sustained and intensified the nature of female migration. Significantly, women have responded to labour markets that specifically demand that they perform their feminized roles of care. This chapter will explore how the notion of feminized work has shaped international and urban-based migrant labour regimes, leading to greater informalization and flexibilization of migrant women's work across Southeast Asia. The governing premise in this chapter is that women do not do unskilled or low-skilled jobs because they are naturally bearers of inferior labour. Rather, the jobs they do are unskilled because women enter them already determined as inferior labourers (Pearson 1997).

The first section discusses contemporary female migrant labour in the context of globalization; the second section will present general trends in migration in and from Southeast Asia; and the final section discusses the employment areas where transnational and rural-urban female migrants are most concentrated: in formal and informal employment within care and entertainment services, and in semi- and low-skilled factory work.

GLOBALIZATION

Globalization has reinforced the movement of skilled and semi-skilled workers who move with foreign direct investment (FDI) flows and multinational investments (International Labour Organization 2002). Tsai and Tsay (2004) further argue that differential levels of economic development in Southeast Asia due to countries' uneven linkages with the global market have spurred different speeds of economic growth. This has led to growing income disparities as well as diverging labour markets that differentiate sending countries from receiving countries even within the region itself. Additionally, better global communications and access to information, and improved transport systems have further stimulated migration.

Transformations in the global economy through FDIs have also ushered in an era of state policies that nurture and protect 'capital', with a concomitant neglect or less protection of labour causing a progressive erosion of labour-protective laws (Ofreneo 2008; Arya and Roy 2006; Symonides 1998). In many industrialized and industrializing countries, this has translated into labour downsizing and the cutting of social benefits to achieve firms' competitive edge to maximize profits from trade in the global export market.

This created the demand for cheap labour with flexible terms of employment especially from impoverished rural sectors and an emerging urban core in developing countries where transnational segments of production have been stationed as new production sites. Gills (2002) points out that multinational companies pursue a stratified rationality of multi-local production where levels of technology and intensity of capital required for each segment of production coincide with the levels of industrialization in the production sites. As a result, de-skilled and fragmented production and assembly work for mass production is located mainly in countries with low wages. Whereas in advanced industrialized countries, financial control, scientific and technological designing, and marketing require a higher level of capital investment and skills, concomitantly shaping and reinforcing a professional and highly-skilled labour force.

Oishi (2007) notes the social effects of these new production regimes in two industrialized countries today, Hong Kong and Singapore, considered as destination countries in Southeast Asia: they both pursued a path of strong export-oriented industrialization, rapid growth in their female labour force participation, and the nuclearization of families. These have led to a strong demand for domestic workers from other Asian countries, such as the Philippines and Indonesia, in order to free working women from daily domestic and care work. Arya and Roy (2006) contend that changes in the international labour market have witnessed a growing demand for traditionally female jobs in the domestic, entertainment and in the labour-intensive sectors of the export garment and textile industries. Additionally, the shift in economic emphasis to the services sector have generally led to the increase in female labour migration, whereas slowdowns in the manufacturing, construction and seafaring industries have reduced the demand for male labour (Gills 2002). Parallel to these movements, women from the rural areas move to cities and peri-urban areas to engage in the informal economy, largely as itinerant vendors, waste pickers, sex workers and domestic workers. They do not have any legal protection both as migrants and as workers and could be vulnerable to even higher forms of exploitation (Piper 2002).

Apart from migrating as industrial labour, women in poorer countries and places also migrate to work as nurses, caregivers, domestic workers, entertainers, sex workers and even as temporary wives in response to the global demand for care, where several tiers or chains of care provision are created and span destination and origin countries and groups across multiple locations. Research in this field has, thus, examined the "global economy of care" (Parrenas 2001), where transnational economic transactions, through networks of recruiters, employers and remittance institutions, harness paid domestic and sexual labour from developing countries. By taking these jobs, migrant women redress the growing "care deficit" in industrializing societies, including a number of Asian cities (Resurreccion, forthcoming).

MIGRATION FLOWS AND TRENDS IN SOUTHEAST ASIA

Labour migration in the whole of Asia has generally shifted from a predominantly Middle East-bound flow to an intra-Asian flow within the past decade (International Labour Organization 2002). The International Labour Organization *Social and Labour Trends 2007* noted that the total number of migrants originating from ASEAN is estimated at about 13.5 million in 2005. Of these, 39 per cent, or 5.3 million people, were in other ASEAN member countries; 26 per cent worked in the United States; 9 per cent in the European Union; and 26 per cent in other regions, primarily the Middle East. Research on migration patterns and flows of Southeast Asia also show that most Southeast Asian states are a combination of both source and destination countries. Table 3.1 shows the migrant populations in countries of the Southeast Asian region.

Several studies further demonstrate this intra-regional pattern and discuss its ramifications. Singapore, Malaysia and Thailand are the main destinations for migrant workers while Indonesia and the Philippines are the principal source countries (Kaur 2007). Data from the International Labour Organization (2007) in Table 3.1 show that the estimated number of Burmese workers in Thailand is as high as 1,382,000 persons while there are about 1,215,000 Indonesian migrants in Malaysia. Malaysian migrants in Singapore number up to 994,000 persons. A common pattern is that the popular destination country often absorbs its migrants from neighbouring countries such as the case of Singapore with large numbers of migrants from Malaysia and Indonesia, and Thailand with peoples migrating from Myanmar, Lao PDR and Cambodia, Malaysia with migrants from Indonesia, and Cambodia with migrants from Vietnam and Thailand. The Philippines is the largest migrant-exporting country in the region, where the number of migrant workers has increased tenfold from between 1974 and 1984, and estimated at 7.8 million Filipinos working in 192 countries in 2003 (Oishi 2005, p. 64). Filipinos work in Southeast Asia, East Asia, the Gulf countries, Europe and North America.

Another recent study on migration patterns comparing the Philippines and Indonesia indicates that the Philippines has a larger outflow of legal migrants (about 800,000) deployed annually whereas Indonesia has a yearly

TABLE 3.1
Bilateral Estimates of Migrant Populations in ASEAN (thousand), 2006

Source	Destination										
	Brunei Darussalam	Cambodia	Indonesia	Lao PDR	Malaysia	Myanmar	Philippines	Singapore	Thailand	Vietnam	ASEAN
Brunei Darussalam	0	0	0	0	0	0	1	0	0	0	1
Cambodia	0	0	0	2	7	0	0	0	232	0	240
Indonesia	6	0	0	0	1,215	0	5	96	1	0	1,323
Lao PDR	0	1	0	0	0	0	0	0	257	0	258
Malaysia	68	1	0	0	0	0	0	994	3	0	1,066
Myanmar	0	0	0	0	92	0	0	0	1,382	0	1,475
Philippines	23	1	0	0	353	0	0	136	3	0	516
Singapore	3	1	0	0	87	0	0	0	2	0	92
Thailand	11	129	0	3	86	0	0	0	0	0	229
Vietnam	0	157	0	15	86	0	1	0	20	0	279
ASEAN	111	290	0	20	1,925	0	8	1,226	1,900	0	5,480

Source: ILO (2007).

deployment of about 300,000. In terms of irregular migration,[1] however, the magnitude is larger in Indonesia than in the Philippines. Much of the irregular outflows from Indonesia are directed to neighbouring Malaysia (Asis 2004, p. 215).

Research on the Mekong Region carried out by the Asian Migrant Centre (AMC) estimates that "there are at least 1.6–2 million migrants in the Mekong Region, most of whom are undocumented". Since governments in the region are not able to track their mobile populations, these then are only rough estimates. The troubled economies of Lao PDR, Cambodia, Vietnam and Myanmar have a "stand-by army" of millions of unemployed. Therefore, there is an intense "labour push" from these countries, resulting in both documented and undocumented migration without government intervention (AMC 2005, p. 2)

In his research on migration in the Mekong Region including Cambodia, the Lao PDR, Myanmar, Thailand, Vietnam and Yunnan Province in Southwest China, Skeldon (2001, p. 30) noted that "present-day population flows are exceedingly complex both in their direction and in their composition. There exist movements from outside the sub-region, and flows within the sub-region itself." By far the most numerous are movements within the sub-region which are dominated by rural-to-urban migrations to the principal centres in each country: Bangkok, Ho Chi Minh City, Ha Noi, Phnom Penh, Yangon, but also a series of provincial cities in Thailand such as Chiang Mai, and around the Thai border towns adjacent to Myanmar, the Lao PDR and Cambodia. "In a very real sense, the rural-to-urban migration fields of many of these centres have extended out across the international boundaries into neighbouring countries" (Skeldon 2001, p. 30). In an earlier study, Skeldon (1998) also says that most of the countries from Southeast Asia are countries with medium levels of urbanization and medium to high urban growth rates such as Brunei Darussalam, Malaysia, Philippines, Indonesia and Thailand. Another group with low levels of urbanization and relatively high urban growth rates include Cambodia, Lao PDR, Myanmar and Vietnam.

A study by Chantavanich (2000) shows four major cross-border flows in the Mekong Region: from Yunnan to the three countries which share its borders; from Myanmar in the west to Thailand; from Vietnam toward Lao PDR and Cambodia; and from Cambodia and Lao PDR to Thailand. Rural-urban mobility has also increased within Thailand and Yunnan, whereas internal mobility in Lao PDR, Cambodia, Myanmar and Vietnam is largely development-driven. Young women and men dominate short-term mobile populations. Although still outnumbered by men, the numbers of women are increasing rapidly and they are moving into a wider range of occupations in view of increased trade, infrastructure development, tourism growth and improved transport links. Most of them move without families. What seems to be happening is the attraction of poorer migrants from less developed areas to emerging centres of industrialization and globalization in the Mekong Region. However, this is not to downplay the fact that others are also on the move, not only the poor.

It should also be noted that many countries in the region are transit countries for migrant workers as in the case of Lao PDR and Thailand. One migration research reveals that Vietnamese and Chinese migrants use Lao PDR as a transit point to other countries. Thailand is also a buffering station for many Vietnamese female migrant workers who temporarily work there to earn enough money to pay for migration fees to higher income countries such as Japan or South Korea (Nguyen 2008). Majority of Indonesian female migrants move to Hong Kong, Malaysia, Taiwan and Singapore (Regional Thematic Working Group on International Migration Including Human Trafficking 2008).

In addition, the increased number of woman migrants in the region in the 1990s, "making female migrants outnumber male ones in Indonesia and the Philippines at the end of the decade", has heated the issue of protection for women migrant workers as their vulnerable situation derives from the fact that they are both "migrants and women" (Chantanavich 2000, p. 125 from Lim and Oishi 1996). Acharya (2003) observes a similar trend in Cambodia where women made up 56 per cent of "very recent" migrants to Phnom Penh, as revealed by the census.[2] This is evidently in response to the opening up of numerous garment and shoe factories in the capital. These began to attract rural women to such jobs in the mid-1990s (Acharya 2003, p. 6).

Having provided broad trends on labour migration within and beyond Southeast Asia, the succeeding sub-sections will attempt to discuss more fully the diversified areas[3] within which female migrants are most concentrated: broadly, in transnational migration for domestic, professional and entertainment services, and in internal rural-urban migration for formal and informal employment in industrial and non-industrial sectors. These two streams of migration have been arbitrarily selected as distinct sections in this chapter since (i) they both represent separate streams in the migration literature that intersect less in writing than in reality and, thus, it may be useful to juxtapose them in one chapter; (ii) migrant women may experience different degrees of insecurity, exploitation, vulnerability and risk in each migration stream; and, (iii) the specific nature and characteristics of capital investments and labour markets may differ in each stream. While all three proposed reasons are important, they will however not be discussed at great length here. Instead, the sections that follow will aim to trace the patterns of female migration in these streams.

TRANSNATIONAL MIGRATION

Domestic Work

The so-called feminization of migration began in the late 1970s when women began being employed as live-in domestic workers in the Middle East. By the mid-1990s, women constituted up to 70 per cent of the migration flow to both the Middle East, and increasingly in East Asian industrializing countries (United Nations Research Institute for Social Development 2005). Domestic workers are usually not fully recognized as workers. A domestic worker "is a wage earner working in a private household, under whatever method and period of payment, who may be employed by one or several employers" (Punpuing 2007). Domestic work is often considered to be unproductive work and economically invisible because of the following: (i) it is work that does not create value because the immediate products are consumed; (ii) it takes place in the 'private' sphere of the household; (iii) it is not reflected in national accounts because it is seen as lying outside the monetary economy; and, (iv) it is perceived as 'women's work' rather than a shared responsibility among women and men and the State (Punpuing 2007, p. 31). Additionally, female migrants fill in the traditional responsibilities of female nationals in households of receiving countries, freeing them up to engage in skilled and professional work, which increases household income and enhances the development capacity of receiving countries. Piper (2005) adds that the significant increases in female labour participation have created a need for social services, especially where mothers of young children work full-time. Migrant domestic workers are high in labour supply and cost less than public care services. They also have very little and arbitrary labour rights, and often depend on the goodwill of their employers.

From the Philippines, the world's largest exporter of labour — about 4.2 to 6.4 million women are working abroad as domestic workers, constituting a huge percentage of the estimated 7–8 million Filipino migrant workers (Wee and Sim 2004). The trend can be traced from the mid-1990s where Filipina migrants often took jobs that require minimal skills or jobs that local women have shunned, thus registering nearly two-thirds of female migrants in domestic work services in Hong Kong, Malaysia and Taiwan, and which did not wane even after the financial crisis that gripped the region in 1997 (United Nations Department of Economic and Social Affairs 2003). In 1998–2006, Khmer domestic workers who migrated to Malaysia numbered 3,705, higher than the number of migrant factory workers at 1,203 (Lee 2007). Punpuing (2007) meantime notes that domestic workers comprised the second largest proportion of irregular migrants (numbering 66,863) next to agriculture, who registered for work permits in Thailand in 2006. Eighty-three per cent came from Myanmar. The reasons for migration that these migrants cited are their persecution as ethnic minorities, severe economic hardship, family pressures to marry, and family conflicts (Archavanitkul 2002 in Punpuing 2007).

Domestic workers, in particular, are difficult to sample as they are spread throughout places as 'invisible workers'. A study on Cambodian female migrants in Malaysia noted that the domestic workers tended to be more vulnerable than those employed in factories or who worked as restaurant waitresses. Their freedom of movement is severely curtailed by their employers on whom they are dependent for food, money, shelter and human company (Lee 2007).

Couple migrants from Lao PDR and Myanmar who work in Thai shrimp farms are often recruited through informal labour recruiters in Bangkok and paid less than their Northeast Thai counterparts who also migrate to work in technology-intensive shrimp farms in the south. Their conditions are likely to vary greatly depending largely on the nature and goodwill of their employers. Some will be well treated and receive living benefits, while others will be shamelessly exploited. Apart from feminized roles in shrimp farms such as feeding, migrant wives are often required to perform domestic services in their employers' households, whereas their husbands work to safeguard shrimp ponds. Both engage in monitoring water quality and harvesting shrimps for the export market. Compared with Lao or Thai migrant couples in shrimp farms, the Burmese couple migrants, however, are much more bonded to their employers because of current policies that require employers to register both themselves and their migrant employees in local immigration offices (Resurreccion and Sajor 2007).

A huge number of migrant women, therefore, tend to be concentrated in non-skilled personal service work. Globally, most women migrants generate incomes by taking up unskilled jobs, often poorly paid and performed in the domestic or private domain of the home. These jobs tend to be devalued economically and looked down upon socially (Piper 2005).

Professional Care and Welfare Services

Globally, skilled women have tended to enter jobs broadly defined as the 'welfare and social professions' (education, health and social work), which are traditionally female jobs (Piper 2005). United Nations Economic and Social Commission for Asia and the Pacific (2002) reports that there will be more female migration in the healthcare sector, such as in nursing and physical therapy. Recourse to recruiting migrant nurses in response to the crisis in the nursing profession has created a global job market especially in the United Kingdom, Ireland, Canada and the United States. The Philippines supplies the majority of nurses working in these countries. Industrializing countries in Southeast Asia do not yet show signs of importing nurses from neighbouring countries. However in Japan, because of decreasing pensions, admitting migrant workers may be a viable option. In the recent Japan-Philippines Economic Partnership Agreement, Japan will accept up to 400 Filipino nurses and 600 caregivers per year for two years once the agreement enters into force (Regional Thematic Working Group on International Migration Including Human Trafficking 2008).[4]

In education, Thailand is currently hosting an increasing number of Filipino teachers of English. There are currently moves to organize groups of Filipino teachers in Thailand whose population is increasing due to the growing number of international schools in Thailand, as well as English teaching programmes in Thai schools. Although no official record register them as a distinct professional category, these teachers are estimated to be about 3,000, and are probably mostly women (Filipino Educators in Thailand 2008). These groups are organized along shared concerns for pedagogy, welfare, experiences of job discrimination, and expat living in Thailand.

Entertainment, Sex Work and Temporary Wives

Many areas of the Thai-Myanmar border have become a destination for migrant workers. One Burmese border town, Tachileik-Mae Sai, is famous for commuting workers crossing into Thailand, which includes women working in entertainment, massage and sex work (Chantavanich 2000). Burmese women living near the border towns of China also explore employment opportunities in these places. A recent study on a Burmese village and migrant remittances revealed the diversity of livelihoods that women (mothers and daughters) have taken as they migrated to Chinese border towns. These livelihoods are listed in Table 3.2.

TABLE 3.2
Types of Work in Kyeigaung, Chinese Border Town,
by Mother and Daughter Migrant Workers

Type of work	Mother migrant worker (10)	Daughter migrant worker (12)
Waitress		1
Shampoo girl		1
Massage girl		1
Cashier	1	2
Domestic worker	3	
Factory worker		1
Tailoring		1
Charcoal smuggler		2
Petty trader	1	
Agriculture worker		2
Temporary wife	3	1
Food shop owner	2	

Source: Din (2006).

According to Din's (2006) study, a broker sold a temporary wife to a Chinese man for whom she performed domestic and sex work. She can be sold to another man after living with her earlier temporary husband for some time. A temporary wife stays in the Chinese town with her temporary husband, receives a wage from her temporary husband, which she usually remits to her family in Myanmar. Many of the temporary wives are married in Myanmar to men who are heavily drug-addicted and are, thus, unable to work for a living. The women have become the *de facto* breadwinners. The market for temporary wives is said to be widespread in border towns in these two countries, and has been viewed as one of the effects of China's increasing male population because of its One Child Policy and cultural norms for son preference. Cases of trafficking women as temporary wives is said to be a pervasive practice as well in these places (Din 2006).

The sex industry in Cambodia is an important employment sector for Vietnamese female migrants. Many women are employed in the sex industry, including massage parlours and dance halls. They are among the most vulnerable migrant workers and are subject to exploitation and extortion, which is amplified by the combination of their profession and irregular status (Regional Thematic Working Group on International Migration Including Human Trafficking 2008; Acharya 2003).

Many Filipina workers also work in entertainment establishments in Japan, where they are recognized as skilled workers under the current Japanese Immigration Control Act and are allowed to remain in the country for up to six months (United Nations Department of Economic and Social Affairs 2003). In Sabah, Malaysia, a recent study of fourteen female Filipino migrants show that like most other female migrants, "the musician, the masseuse and the manager constitute part of the feminisation of labour in which women have come to dominate overseas migration flows working in areas linked with reproductive activities such as domestic service, entertainment and sex work" (Hilsdon 2007, p. 196). The study further challenges the notion that economic motivations are distinct and separate from marriage aspirations of female migrants, contrary to earlier studies that underscore economic motivations as largely driving women to migrate overseas.

RURAL-URBAN MIGRATION

Rural areas in Southeast Asia are experiencing rapid and far-reaching changes. Studies have shown that occupations and livelihoods in the countryside are diversifying. Occupational multiplicity is becoming more common and more pronounced. The balance of household income is shifting from farm to non-farm. Livelihoods and poverty are becoming de-linked from land and from agriculture. Livelihoods are becoming de-localized and multi-local, while simultaneously, the average age of farmers is rising and more young people are seeking work beyond their rural villages (Tacoli 1998; Rigg 1998, 2003; De Haan and Rogaly 2002; Elmhirst 2008; Resurreccion and Van Khanh 2007; Bryceson et al. 2000; Lynch 2005). Female migrants also respond to similar employment opportunities, as those discussed in the previous section on transnational migration. Differences may possibly reside in the nature and degree of insecurity, vulnerability and exploitation that they face and experience in the hands of employers, police and immigration authorities, their volume of remitted earnings, and in their relations with those they left behind. For instance, in a recent study mentioned earlier, it was discovered that in Thailand's southern technology-intensive export shrimp farms, Burmese migrants were generally more bonded to their employers than Northern Thai migrants due to more stringent immigration policies currently in place in Thailand. Moreover, Northern Thai migrant women had greater latitude for engaging in multiple livelihoods (apart from shrimp farming) compared with their Burmese counterparts (Resurreccion and Sajor 2007). Immigration policies and issues aside and possibly for future study elsewhere, the following sub-sections discuss the ramifications of female rural-urban migration in some parts of Southeast Asia.

Garment and Textile Factories

The sharp growth of the tourism and manufacturing industries in Thailand has prompted more than 1.3 million women from rural areas to move to urban, municipal areas (Gender and Development Research Institute 2007). Among the total labourers working in these industries, 57.1 per cent are women while men account for less than 42.9 per cent (National Statistical Office 2005). Present-day disparities between urban and rural areas drive rural Thai women to migrate to urban areas, because of the considerable demand for unskilled and low-paid labour particularly associated with female labour (Han and Resurreccion 2008). A study on skill development in Thailand some years ago revealed that the top three manufacturing establishments that contributed a huge share of the Kingdom's GDP were food processing, garment and textile industries where women workers are concentrated (Suriyisarn and Resurreccion 2003; see Manufacturing Establishments nos. 1, 4, and 7 in Table 3.3). Most of these women workers are probably migrants from other Thai provinces who have come to seek wage employment in Bangkok, and from the figures in the table, demonstrate that female labour has contributed significantly to Thailand's GDP and to maintaining the low cost of industrial production.[5]

In a study on the adoption of new agricultural technologies in Cambodia (Resurreccion and Sajor 2008), it was found that beginning in their thirties, more men than women work away from their villages to perform non-farm occupations in construction sites. It is also equally noteworthy that there are more women than men up to age twenty-nine who work outside their villages. The study discovered that these young women were employed by garment factories owned by Chinese businessmen in nearby provincial towns. In contrast from the age of thirty onwards, there is a deep plunge in the percentage of women who work as labour migrants. This seems to indicate that in view of preference for young female labour by the urban labour market, older women have then become the farm mainstays in their villages. Figure 3.1 presents this differentiation among ages and genders.

The gender and age differentials in non-farm employment indicate that new meanings regarding the position of women as farmers and factory workers are being re-worked along age and life cycle parameters.

Studies in Thailand and Cambodia demonstrate the propensity of rural women to respond to urban employment opportunities and that their

TABLE 3.3
Employment of Women and Men in Top Seven Manufacturing Establishments, Thailand, 1999

Manufacturing Establishment	Number of Establishments	Percentage Share of Manufacturing in GDP*	Male Labour	Female Labour	Total
1. Manufacture of food products and beverages	3,001	18.2	144,005 (38%)	235,627 (62%)	379,632 (100%)
2. Manufacture of other non-metallic mineral products	2,195	4.3	90,012 (69%)	40,812 (31%)	130,824 (100%)
3. Manufacture of fabricated metal products, except machinery and equipment	2,139	0.9	65,591 (62%)	41,251 (38%)	106,842 (100%)
4. Manufacture of wearing apparel dressing and dyeing of fur	1,928	11	21,955 (16%)	119,349 (84%)	141,304 (100%)
5. Manufacture of rubber and plastic products	1,761	3	78,920 (45%)	95,840 (55%)	174,760 (100%)
6. Manufacture of furniture	1,713	1.3	69,491 (45%)	83,752 (55%)	153,243 (100%)
7. Manufacture of textiles	1,316	6.7	62,600 (31%)	138,572 (69%)	201,172 (100%)
Total		1,435,369 (million baht) 100%	532,574 (41%)	755,203 (59%)	1,287,777 (100%)

Note: * NESDB Gross Domestic Product at Current Market Prices, 1999.
Source: Thailand National Statistical Office, Labour Force Survey, 1999*b*.

FIGURE 3.1

Percentage of Adult Labour Performing Non-Farm Occupations Outside Villages by Gender (N = 479)

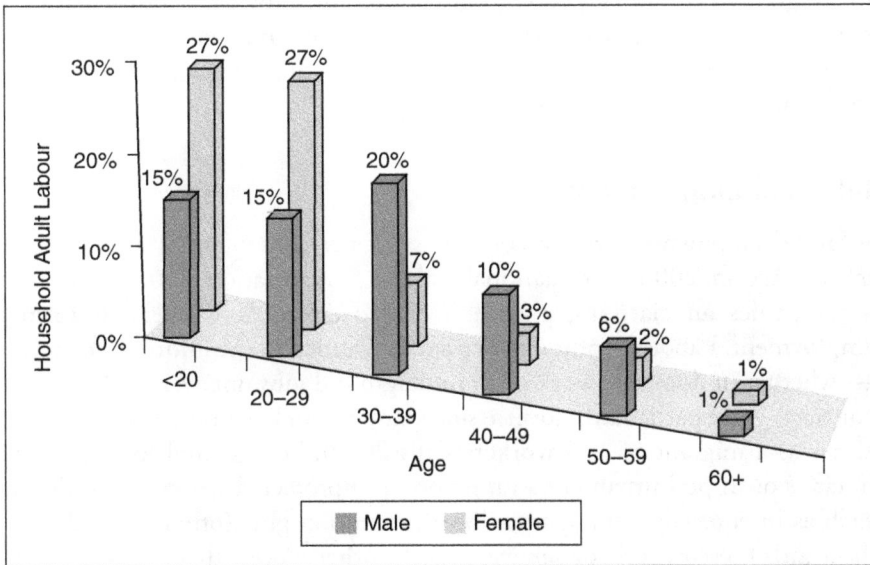

Source: Resurreccion and Sajor (2008).

migration may yield both positive and negative consequences (De Haan 2000). While female migrants may work in key revenue-generating industries that enable them access to better incomes, social experiences of living in the city may place them at greater risk. A few cases demonstrate this. Ties with kin and those left behind may provide the informal support networks for childcare that female migrants may need to navigate living in the city. Adversely, these same ties may serve to disfavour Indonesian female migrant returnees to the rural areas over male returnees during the Asian financial crisis in the late 1990s (Silvey and Elmhirst 2003). Another recent study on female migration and domestic violence in Bangkok cited social isolation and poverty as factors that constrained women from escaping violent relationships with partners. These women had severed ties with family members in the provinces due to their inability to remit earnings for children they had left in the care of elderly parents and relatives while they worked in Bangkok. This brought them a sense of social isolation especially in the face of domestic violence (Han and Resurreccion 2008). In Cambodia, older women are increasingly becoming farm mainstays, as younger women and men move to work outside their villages. This suggests that farming may assume an increasingly reproductive function by providing care, safety nets and food security in the countryside for migrant and mobile people. Agriculture also provides a broad base for semi-skilled migrants who work in urban labour markets such as in the growing garment industry. Feminization of agriculture has then given way to feminization of migrant labour in cities.

Informal Employment

Informal employment today comprises 63 per cent of total employment in ASEAN in 2006 (International Labour Organization 2007). This rise accompanies an alarming plunge in the decrease of workers in formal employment. Labour conditions of migrant women in the informal economy — whether in domestic work or in underground jobs ungoverned by a legal contract — are particularly adverse since they do not have any legal protection either as a migrant or as a worker (Gills 2002). Young rural women work in cities or in peri-urban areas under often unprotected working conditions such as in entertainment spots as beer promotion girls (often referred to as 'beer girls'), escort girls or sex workers. In other places, they work as waste pickers and recyclers and small transport operators (Resurreccion and Van Khanh 2007; Ofreneo 2008).

Lee (2007) points out that rural women dominate rural-urban migration in Cambodia, many of whom work as hairdressers, petrol and cigarette sellers, manicurists, shop assistants, and fruit vendors. There are an estimated 4,000 beer promotion girls in Cambodia, most falling between 20–29 years old. They work in beer gardens, karaoke bars, nightclubs and soup shops. Beer promotion is associated with sex work, and beer promoters as 'indirect sex workers' are often subject to verbal abuse and sexual harassment. Since they work on a commission-basis earning a basic salary of US$50 per month, most usually end up selling beer at all costs even if it means having to engage in sex work.

Rural women from the Red River Delta working in the city of Hanoi as waste pickers live in crowded hostels, where they sleep on floor mats and where it is unbearably hot and dusty during the summer and very cold in the winter. They live in the city for eight months yearly and return to Nam Dinh Province during the peak labour periods of rice planting and harvesting. The migrant women work within an exclusive and a complex network of co-villagers in the waste recycling industry. Their husbands are left behind to farm their small landholdings. The younger women are the waste pickers and scavengers, while the older, more well-off women and men are buyers of recyclable waste which, in turn, are sold to bigger recycling plants (Resurreccion and Van Khanh 2007). Waste picking is considered an exclusively feminine job in Vietnam.

Couple migrants from rural areas in Northern Thailand who work in the shrimp farms of the city of Surat Thani, Southern Thailand, reside and work in these farms. For monitoring water quality, feeding and guarding the shrimp ponds from theft, they earn a couple wage that is smaller than two individual wages, and have access to lodging and a food allowance. However, migrant wives are expected to perform domestic work apart from feeding the shrimps and employers require children older than five years to be sent back to their villages of origin (Resurreccion and Sajor 2007). This is the case where the boundary dividing production and domestic work blur because of the informality of the employment arrangement and that a migrant wife is governed by social norms of domesticity. It draws attention to the flexibilization of work largely associated with female labour.

CONCLUSION

The governing premise in the concluding remarks comes from Pearson (1997): women do not do unskilled or low-skilled jobs because they are naturally bearers of inferior labour. Rather, the jobs they do are unskilled because women enter them already determined as inferior labourers.

What then do these gender, employment and migration trends in Southeast Asia tell us in light of this premise?

First, migrant women from peripheral countries and the rural areas are slotting themselves into occupations that provide personal services such as domestic work, beauty care and entertainment, or in informal employment sectors of waste recycling and beer promotion especially in the urban core of developing and industrializing countries and their emerging peri-urban areas. They are also concentrated in manufacturing establishments that generate huge profits through low or semi skilled-driven mass production and assembly plants located in peripheral countries where labour costs are specifically low.

Second, migrant women are generally located in occupations where they experience degrees of de-skilling, insecurity, risk, vulnerability, social isolation because of weak and unstable social networks and where their work is often sexualized, feminized and as a result, undervalued.

Third, female migrant work is often regarded as flexible, thus subjected to arbitrary terms of employment that blur the boundary between private care and public production services.

Fourth, migration for women can both be positive and negative depending on the contexts of their host societies, working conditions, social support networks and relations and obligations to families left behind; thus, they should be understood more holistically against such contexts. Moreover, the implications of migrating to abandon one sector, notably agriculture, has created an emerging layer of older female farmers who provide food security and a broad reproductive platform from which other female and male migrants are freed to take up non-farm opportunities beyond their rural villages. The feminization of agriculture has stimulated the feminization of labour migration.

This chapter has attempted to provide a broad overview of trends on gendered migration and labour employment in Southeast Asia. Specific contemporary concerns and developments around this theme are worth exploring in future research. These are listed below:

- The implications of a new stream of migrant returnees as a result of this global financial crisis and its massive layoffs.
- The heteronormative bias is much of gender and migration studies: studies on male physicians who enter female-dominated jobs such as nursing, gay or lesbian migrant workers and how they negotiate their identities and employment with host societies, institutions and left-behind kin have yet to pervade migration research.
- Men are now the left behind in gender and migration research: both in terms of subject focus and the paucity of research on men actually left behind by migrant women and the challenges with changing masculinities.
- The effects on migrants' gendered re-integration in communities.
- Lessons from non-governmental organizations in their efforts to empower migrant women.
- Policy discourses and processes on migration in receiving and sending countries and the responsiveness of ASEAN and other multilateral organizations to gender in migration issues.

Notes

1. Irregular migration is often referred to as 'illegal migration' and subsequently migrants are labelled as 'illegal migrants'. This language casts migrants as violators and obfuscates the fact that other actors and institutions could be violators and that migrants could be their victims (Asis 2004, p. 204).

2.   The demographics in Cambodia, however, indicate a slightly higher number of women, especially female-headed households, because of the high number of male deaths during the war-torn years.

3.   Recent discussions on the feminization of migration draw attention to the diversified and stratified nature of women's migration: they have several types of employment in different labour markets, and, these types of employment are hierarchically positioned according to the social status, skills, assets of female migrants (Regional Thematic Working Group on International Migration Including Human Trafficking 2008).

4.   On the other hand, declining pensions and retirement benefits in East Asia have stimulated migration of the elderly to the Philippines, Thailand and Vietnam, where care, real estate and retirement services are increasingly becoming a lucrative economic niche.

5.   In manufacturing, women generally earn a monthly wage of 6,700 THB (approx. US$192), whereas men earn a monthly wage of 8,500 THB (approx. US$244) for the same category of jobs (National Statistical Office 2000).

References

Acharya, Sarthi. "Labour Migration in the Transitional Economies of Southeast Asia". Working Paper on Migration and Urbanization. United Nations Economic and Social Commission for Asia and the Pacific (UNESCAP), Bangkok, 2003.

Asian Migration Centre (AMC). *Migration in the Greater Mekong Subregion: Regional Synthesis*. Hong Kong: Asian Migration Centre, 2005.

Asis, Maruja M.B. "Borders, Globalization and Irregular Migration in Southeast Asia". In *International Migration in Southeast Asia*, edited by A. Ananta and E.N. Arifin. Singapore: Institute of Southeast Asian Studies, 2004.

Bryceson, Deborah F., Cristobal Kay, and Jos Mooij, eds. *Disappearing Peasantries: Rural Labour in Africa, Asia and Latin America*. London: ITDG Publishing, 2000.

Cadias, Abel C. First Filipino Educators Conference in Thailand, 2008 <http://www.filipinoeducatorsinthailand.com/synopsis-report-1st-chiangmai-chiangrai-filipino-educators-conference/> (accessed 1 December 2008).

Chantavanich, Supang. *Mobility and HIV/AIDS in the Greater Mekong Subregion*. Bangkok, Thailand: Asian Research Center for Migration and Asian Development and United Nations Development Programme, 2000.

De Haan, Arjan. *Migrants, Livelihoods and Rights: The Relevance of Migration in Development Policies*. Working Paper no. 4. London: Social Development Department, Department for International Development (DFID), 2000.

De Haan, A. and B. Rogaly. "Introduction: Migrant Workers and Their Role in Rural Change". *Journal of Development Studies* 38, no. 5 (2002): 1–14.

Din, Kaythi Min. "The Social Effects of Remittances on Migrant Households in the Myanmar-China Border". Master of Science Thesis. Gender and Development Studies, Asian Institute of Technology, 2006.

Elmhirst, R. "Multi-local Livelihoods, Natural Resource Management and Gender in Upland Indonesia". In *Gender and Natural Resource Management. Livelihoods, Mobility and Interventions*, edited by B. Resurreccion and R. Elmhirst. London and Ottawa: Earthscan and IDRC, 2008.

Gender and Development Research Institute (GDRI) 2001. *Status of Women in Thailand: An Overview* <http://www. gdrif.org> (accessed 20 July 2006).

Gills, Dong-Sook. "Neo-liberal Economic Globalisation and Women in Asia: Introduction". In *Women and Work in Globalising Asia*, edited by D.-S. Gills, and N. Piper. London: Routledge, 2002.

Han, C. and B. Resurreccion. "Struggling Alone: Gender, Migration and Domestic Violence among Thai Women in Bangkok". *Asian Journal of Women's Studies* 14, no. 1 (2008): 34–39.

Hilsdon, Anne-Marie. "The Musician, the Masseuse and the Manager: Sexy Mothers in Sabah". In *Working and Mothering in Asia: Images, Ideologies and Identities*, edited by T.W. Devasahayam and B.S.A. Yeoh. Singapore and Copenhagen: National University of Singapore Press and Nordic Institute of Asian Studies Press, 2007.

International Labour Organization (ILO). "Asian Labour Migration: Issues and Challenges in an Era of Globalization". International Migration Papers 57. Geneva: ILO, 2002.

————. *Social and Labour Trends in ASEAN 2007*. Geneva: International Labour Organization, 2007.

Kaur, A. "Migration Matters in the Asia-Pacific Region: Immigration 135 Frameworks, Knowledge Workers and National Policies". *International Journal on Multicultural Studies* 9, no. 2 (2007): 135–57.

Lee, C.C. "Female Labour Migration in Cambodia". In *Perspectives on Gender and Migration: From the Regional Seminar on Strengthening the Capacity of National Machineries for Gender Equality to Shape Migration Policies and Protect Migrant Women, Bangkok, 22–24 November 2006*, pp. 6–19. Bangkok: United Nations Economic and Social Commission for Asia and the Pacific, 2007.

Lynch, Kenneth. *Rural-urban Interaction in the Developing World*. London: Routledge, 2005.

National Statistics Office (NSO). *Labour Force Survey*. Bangkok: NSO, 2000.

————. *Core Economic Indicators of Thailand*. Bangkok: NSO, 2005.

Nguyen, Thi Hai Yen. *Understanding Gendered Transnational Community Identity of the Vietnamese Service Workers in Bangkok*. Master of Science Thesis. Gender and Development Studies, Asian Institute of Technology, 2008.

Ofreneo, Rosalinda. "Confronting Neoliberal Globalization: Bridging the Gender and Formal/Informal Divide in Labour Movements within ASEAN". Paper presented at the Conference on Asian Feminisms Confronts Neo-liberalism,

Fundamentalisms and Conflict. Kartini Network on Women and Gender Institutes in Asia, Bali, Indonesia, 3–5 November 2008.

Parrenas, R.S. "Mothering from a Distance: Emotions, Gender, and Inter-generational Relations in Filipino Transnational Families". *Feminist Studies* 7, no. 2 (2001): 361–90.

Pearson, Ruth. "Nimble Fingers Revisited: Reflections on Women and Third World Industrialisation in the Late Twentieth Century". In *Feminist Visions of Development*, edited by C. Jackson and R. Pearson. London: Routledge, 1997.

Piper, Nicola. "Global Labour Markets and National Responses: Legal Regimes Governing Female Migrant Workers in Japan". In *Women and Work in Globalising Asia*, edited by D.-S. Gills and N. Piper. London: Routledge, 2002.

Punpuing, Sureeporn. "Female Migration in Thailand: A Study of Migrant Domestic Workers". In *Perspectives on Gender and Migration: From the Regional Seminar on Strengthening the Capacity of National Machineries for Gender Equality to Shape Migration Policies and Protect Migrant Women, Bangkok, 22–24 November 2006*, pp. 22–44. Bangkok: United Nations Economic and Social Commission for Asia and the Pacific, 2007.

Regional Thematic Working Group on International Migration Including Human Trafficking. *Situation Report on International Migration in East and South-east Asia*. Bangkok: International Organization for Migration, 2008.

Resurreccion, Bernadette. "Gender, Migration and Social Reproduction in the Mekong Region". *Asian and Pacific Migration Journal* 18, no. 1 (2009): 101–22.

Resurreccion, Bernadette and Edsel Sajor. "Not a Real Worker: (Re)productions of Gender, Identity and Place in Technology-intensive Shrimp Farming, Thailand". Paper presented at the International Workshop on Female Labor Migration in Globalizing Asia. Asia Research Institute, National University of Singapore, Singapore, 13–14 September 2007.

———. "Performative Innovation: Gendered Practices of Adopting the System of Rice Intensification (SRI) in Cambodia". Paper presented at the Conference on Asian Feminisms Confronts Neo-liberalism, Fundamentalisms and Conflict. Kartini Network on Women and Gender Institutes in Asia, Bali, Indonesia, 3–5 November 2008.

Resurreccion, B. and H.T.V. Khanh. "Able to Come and Go: Reproducing Gender in the Red River Delta". *Population, Space and Place* 13, no. 3 (2007): 211–24.

Rigg, J. "Rural-urban Interactions, Agriculture and Wealth: A Southeast Asian Perspective". *Progress in Human Geography* 24, no 4 (1998): 497–522.

———. *Southeast Asia: The Human Landscape of Modernization and Development*. London and New York: Routledge, 2003.

Skeldon, R. "Urbanization and Migration in the ESCAP Region". *Asia-Pacific Population Journal* 13, no. 1 (1998): 3–24 <http://www.unescap.org/esid/psis/population/journal/articles/1998/v13n1a1.htm> (accessed 4 January 2009).

———. *Population Mobility and HIV Vulnerability in South East Asia: An Assessment and Analysis*. Bangkok: United Nations Development Programme, 2001.

Silvey, R. and R. Elmhirst. "Emerging Social Capital: Women Workers and Rural-Urban Networks in Indonesia's Crisis". *World Development* 31, no. 5 (2003): 865–79.

Suriyisarn, Busakorn and Bernadette Resurreccion. *Action Research: Gender Dimension of Skills Development in Vocational Training in Thailand*. Bangkok: International Labour Organization, 2003.

Symonides, Janusz. *Human Rights: New Dimensions and Challenges*. Dartmouth: Ashgate, 1998.

Tsai, Pan-Long and Ching-Lung Tsay. "Foreign Direct Investment and International Labour Migration in Economic Development: Indonesia, Malaysia, Philippines and Thailand". In *International Migration in Southeast Asia*, edited by A. Ananta and N. Arifin. Singapore: Institute of Southeast Asian Studies, 2004.

United Nations Department of Economic and Social Affairs. *Levels and Trends of International Migration to Selected Countries in Asia*. New York: United Nations Department of Economic and Social Affairs, 2003.

United Nations Economic and Social Commission for Asia and the Pacific (UNESCAP). *International Migration: An Emerging Opportunity for the Socio-economic Development of the ESCAP Region*. Social Policy Paper no. 6. Bangkok: UNESCAP, 2002.

United Nations Research Institute for Social Development (UNRISD). *Gender Equality: Striving for Justice in an Unequal World*. Geneva: UNRISD, 2005.

Wee, Vivienne and Amy Sim. "Transnational Networks in Female Labour Migration". In *International Migration in Southeast Asia*, edited by A. Ananta and N. Arifin. Singapore: Institute of Southeast Asian Studies, 2004.

4

HAS GENDER ANALYSIS BEEN MAINSTREAMED IN THE STUDY OF SOUTHEAST ASIAN POLITICS?

Susan Blackburn

INTRODUCTION

About twenty years ago, some of us feminist scholars became exasperated at the neglect of gender in writing on Southeast Asian politics and held a conference at Monash University to discuss the matter. As women, we were offended by the invisibility of our sex in political science, and by the discipline's failure to acknowledge that its concepts (for example, class) were gendered.[1] The conference in 1987 gave rise to a book edited by Maila Stivens entitled *Why Gender Matters in Southeast Asian Politics*,[2] which launched an attack on the political science discipline for its neglect of gender as far as writing on Southeast Asia was concerned. My chapter in that volume analysed a number of mainstream politics texts on Southeast Asia and noted their abysmal lack of interest in anything relating to gender. Two decades later, I am revisiting this question to see what, if anything, has changed. When we held our earlier conference, feminism had only just begun to influence the study of Southeast Asia.[3] Many feminist works relevant to Southeast Asian politics have now been written, and I will refer to some of them in what follows. Can we now see their impact on mainstream politics writing?

The task I posed for myself was to examine some mainstream political writing about Southeast Asia in the last five to ten years, roughly since the Asian financial crisis which had considerable political effects in some countries. The question I asked was: If you wanted to find out about Southeast Asian politics during the last decade, what general books (that is, not specifically about women) would you turn to and would they tell you anything about women or gender? Since there are very few general books on Southeast Asian politics, I also chose to look at some political science works on the three Southeast Asian countries with which I am most familiar: Indonesia, Malaysia and Vietnam. I chose only scholarly works, so as to gain a better insight into the discipline of political science, and I aimed to include authors from both inside and outside the region. Although all the books are in English, they give a reasonable coverage of scholarly writing because local scholars contribute to books in English to reach a wider market. The following tables (see Tables 4.1–4.4) divide the books I will be analysing into four categories: general works and those on the politics of the three Southeast Asian countries I have selected.

This makes a total of sixteen books, too many to examine here in great detail. My aim is to see what general statements can be made about gender mainstreaming in this literature. The authors of these books come from Australia, North America and Europe as well as from Southeast Asia, and while the vast majority of authors are men, women are also represented.

TABLE 4.1
General Works on Southeast Asian Politics

Book title	Author/editor	Publication date	Place and publisher
Southeast Asian Affairs 2008	Daljit Singh and Tin Maung Maung Than, eds.	2008	Singapore: Institute of Southeast Asian Studies
Government and Politics in Southeast Asia	John Funston, ed.	2001	London: Zed Books
The Political Economy of Southeast Asia	Gary Rodan, Kevin Hewison, and Richard Robison, eds.	2006	Melbourne: Oxford University Press
Politics in Southeast Asia: Democracy or Less	William Case	2002	London: Zed Books

TABLE 4.2
Books on Indonesian Politics

Book title	Author/editor	Publication date	Place and publisher
Politics of Indonesia	Damien Kingsbury	2005	Melbourne: Oxford University Press
Elections in Indonesia: The New Order and Beyond	Hans Antlov and Sven Cederroth, eds.	2004	London: RoutledgeCurzon
The Indonesian Parliament and Democratization	Patrick Ziegenhain	2008	Singapore: Institute of Southeast Asian Studies
Autonomy and Disintegration in Indonesia	Damien Kingsbury and Harry Aveling, eds.	2003	London: RoutledgeCurzon
Local Power and Politics in Indonesia: Decentralisation and Democratisation	Edward Aspinall and Greg Fealy, eds.	2003	Singapore: Institute of Southeast Asian Studies

TABLE 4.3
Books on Malaysian Politics

Book title	Author/editor	Publication date	Place and publisher
Protest and Possibilities: Civil Society and Coalitions for Political Change in Malaysia	Meredith Weiss	2006	Stanford: Stanford University Press
The State of Malaysia: Ethnicity, equity and reform	Edmund Terence Gomez, ed.	2004	London: RoutledgeCurzon
Malaysia: Recent Trends and Challenges	Saw Swee-Hock and K. Kesavapany, eds.	2006	Singapore: Institute of Southeast Asian Studies
Democracy in Malaysia: Discourses and Practices	Francis Loh Kok Wah and Khoo Boo Teik, eds.	2002	Richmond: Curzon

TABLE 4.4
Books on Vietnamese Politics

Book title	Author/editor	Publication date	Place and publisher
The Power of Everyday Politics: How Vietnamese Peasants Transformed National Policy	Benedict J. Tria Kerkvliet	2005	Ithaca: Cornell University Press
Rethinking Vietnam	Duncan McCargo, ed.	2004	London: RoutledgeCurzon
Vietnam's New Order	Stephanie Balme and Mark Sidel, eds.	2006	London: PalgraveMacmillan

To obtain comparability in establishing whether these works had mainstreamed gender, I asked the following general questions:

- Is "women" or "gender" in the index?
- Are women mentioned in the book? (Sometimes the index does not pick this up.)
- Are any feminist writings consulted? (Bibliographies can be revealing.)
- How is politics conceived and what are the political questions being addressed? This is important since the very conventional way of studying politics, restricting it to elites and formal institutions, is a sure way of avoiding discussion on gender. Analysts who see politics in a wider sense are more likely to see the relevance of gender.

To foreshadow my conclusions in terms of gender content, the results of my analysis of the books I have chosen are generally disappointing, but occasionally surprising and gratifying.

My analysis of gender is admittedly "female-biased": it tends to focus on looking for the women rather than building an analysis on the fact that both masculinity and femininity are involved in gender construction. Strange as it may seem, considering the male domination of the public sphere, the discussion of masculinity in Southeast Asian politics is at a very early stage: we have still to see analysis of how the way in which masculinities are constructed affects politics. In his study of the Military Academy in the Philippines, Alfred McCoy (1995, p. 694, as cited in Sears 2007, p. 58) made an observation that might well be taken on board by political scientists studying male-dominated institutions in general:

> This essay is informed by an awareness that its actors are indeed male. It does not assume that their actions, undefined and undifferentiated in a gender sense, somehow represent a universal standard of human behaviour. Reading maleness into a national history dominated by men constitutes, I would argue, a significant corrective to a certain kind of gender bias.[4]

One can scarcely avoid acknowledging the particular construction of masculinity in a military academy; as yet there has been little attention paid to masculinity in other male-dominated institutions like political parties in Southeast Asia. At present, it is enough to gain acknowledgement that political institutions and processes are gendered. Since they are gendered by men in their own favour, it is women who become invisible and therefore require immediate attention.

WHAT DOES THE INDEX REVEAL?

Almost all of the books examined have an index. (The exception is *Southeast Asian Affairs 2008* which is understandable since it is really an annual periodical.) Seven of the remaining fifteen books have no index entries for women or gender, which suggests that the concepts are not considered important by the authors or editors. Table 4.5 lists these books.

TABLE 4.5
Books that Lack Index Entries on Women/Gender

Author/editor(s)	Title
Funston, ed. (2001)	*Government and Politics in Southeast Asia*
Gomez, ed. (2004)	*The State of Malaysia*
Balme and Sidel, eds. (2006)	*Vietnam's New Order*
Kingsbury (2005)	*Politics of Indonesia*
Antlov and Cederroth, eds. (2004)	*Elections in Indonesia*
Ziegenhain (2008)	*The Indonesian Parliament and Democratization*
Kingsbury and Aveling, eds. (2003)	*Autonomy and Disintegration in Indonesia*

The other eight books have entries for women but it is very rare to find "gender" in the index (Aspinall and Fealy (2003) have an entry for "gender mainstreaming"), reflecting the lack of gender analysis to be found in these publications.

WHAT DO BIBLIOGRAPHIES REVEAL?

I ask this question in order to investigate whether the authors are reading and utilizing any of the insights to be gained from the growing number of feminist works being written about Southeast Asian politics. Some books have consolidated bibliographies, while some edited works have individual lists of references for each chapter. I consulted both to draw up the following table (see Table 4.6), listing the authors or editors of books according to how many feminist works were included in their bibliographies.

These results indicate to me that few authors have read or thought important anything written specifically about women in relation to Southeast Asian politics.

TABLE 4.6
Bibliographies

Bibliography contains no feminist works or works on women	Bibliography contains less than three such works	Bibliography contains more than three such works
Balme and Sidel, eds. (2006)	Rodan, Hewison, and Robison, eds. (2006)	Aspinall and Fealy, eds. (2003)
Case (2002)	Kingsbury (2005)	Weiss (2006)
Ziegenhain (2008)	Antlov and Cederroth, eds. (2004)	Loh and Khoo, eds. (2002)
Southeast Asian Affairs 2008	Kingsbury and Aveling, eds. (2003)	Kerkvliet (2005)
Gomez, ed. (2004)	McCargo, ed. (2004)	
Saw and Kesavapany, eds. (2006)	Funston, ed. (2001)	

DOES THE TEXT DEAL WITH WOMEN/GENDER AT ALL?

One may, of course, be unwilling to accept the index as the final arbiter of whether women are discussed in these books. Moreover I wanted to see how women or gender were mentioned or ignored, so I looked more closely at the texts. If the book was a compilation of chapters on different Southeast Asian countries, I examined chapters dealing with Southeast Asia in general and on Indonesia, Malaysia and Vietnam in particular. Table 4.7 summarises the contexts in which women/gender is mentioned.

TABLE 4.7
How Women/Gender is Raised (listed by author/editor)

Books without any mention of women/ gender	Books which mention women and in what context
Southeast Asian Affairs 2008	Funston, eds. (2001). Chapter by Smith (p. 84) has a paragraph on political status of women in Indonesia. Chapter by Funston (p. 167) contains a paragraph saying women are politically under-represented in Malaysia. Vasakul's chapter (p. 380) on Vietnam notes that the Vietnamese constitution emphasizes equal rights for men and women. Conclusion by Funston (p. 411) notes that Southeast Asia is a region noted for the 'relatively high status of women'.
Kingsbury and Aveling, eds. (2003)	Rodan et al., eds. (2006). Chapter by Beresford (p. 218) notes that women are in a majority in categories of people largely excluded from state power in Vietnam. Deyo (pp. 290–01) mentions that young women in manufacturing industries in Southeast Asia have protested against working conditions but without much success.
Balme and Sidel, eds. (2006)	Case (2002) (pp. 31 and 44) mentions Dharma Wanita, the New Order organization for bureaucrats' wives. He mentions that some women were involved in the 1998 protests against Soeharto (p. 61) and that there was controversy over a female president (p. 69). He notes that in Malaysia, women's groups appeared in 1980s and 1990s (p. 126) and that UMNO has a women's wing (pp. 112–13).
	Kingsbury (2005). On p. 107 in discussion of the impact of the Asian financial crisis in Indonesia, he notes women were particularly affected by unemployment and poverty. He mentions the rape of Chinese Indonesian women in May 1998 (pp. 10 and 179). Page 312 mentions Islamic opposition to Megawati becoming president because she is a woman.

TABLE 4.7   (*Cont'd*)

Books without any mention of women/ gender	Books which mention women and in what context
	Antlov and Cederroth, eds. (2004). In his chapter, Antlov (pp. 119 and 130) mentions women as voters, and observes a gender gap in 1997 elections (p. 115) when women he interviewed objected to the government's pressure to have contraceptive injections. Haris (p. 69) notes Islamic debate as to whether Indonesia could have a female president.
	In a general discussion of the representative function of parliaments, Ziegenhain (2008) notes that ideally equal gender representation should be targeted (pp. 36–37). On p. 116, he observes that the 1999 elections were not fully representative because, among other things, 92 per cent of those elected were men.
	Aspinall and Fealy, eds. (2003). A chapter by Hana Satriyo specifically addresses the impact of decentralization on women. Chapter by Ryaas Rasyid (p. 65) notes that since 1998, more women have been elected as local leaders. Antlov's chapter (p. 85) suggests that seats might be reserved in village councils for women and *adat* (cultural) minorities. Colongon (p. 98) also notes that women's participation in local governments 'remains unacceptably low'.
	In her analysis of NGOs in Malaysia, Weiss (2006) deals with women's groups and discusses their role in democratization more generally.
	Gomez, ed. (2004). Case (p. 33) notes that the new opposition movement in Malaysia includes women's groups. He mentions that the working class has been fragmented by gender as well as ethnicity (p. 39) and that the Islamic party PAS alienated those 'geared to women's issues'. In her discussion of the political role of intellectuals in Malaysia, Derichs mentions the success of women's groups in adding the term "gender" to an article of the federal constitution on discrimination. She also notes that by the late 1990s, "the support of women was becoming important in federal and state elections" (p. 118). Welsh mentions the formation of UMNO Puteri in 2002 (p. 143) and notes that women's groups joined protests in 1998 (p. 131).

TABLE 4.7 *(Cont'd)*

Books without any mention of women/ gender	Books which mention women and in what context
	Saw and Kesavapany, eds. (2006). Chong (p. 39) mentions that UMNO in 2004 endorsed principles including protection of rights of minority groups and women. He discusses Sisters In Islam as an example of new political space opening up for NGOs (p. 42). In his analysis of 2004 elections, Gomez says PAS alienated two important groups: women and youth, and UMNO moved to cultivate the support of women. He mentions women candidates in the 2004 election, and establishment of young women's wings by UMNO and MIC (pp. 94–95). Hamid (p. 114) mentions that PAS youth called for the formation of a women's youth section. In his chapter on Barisan Nasional, Kling (p. 188) mentions women's wings of parties.
	Loh and Khoo, eds. (2002). Maznah Mohamad contributed a chapter on the contribution of women's groups to democratization in Malaysia. Writing about Muslim politics, Hussein (p. 98) discusses PAS attitudes to women candidates. Discussing political NGOs, Hassan (pp. 209–11) mentions SIS and Tenaganita and that SUARAM addresses themes that include rights of women.
	Kerkvliet (2005). His methodology included interviews with 81 villagers, about a third of whom were women, and he quotes them quite often and is alert to discussion of gender impact of collectivization and decollectivization of land in Vietnam.
	McCargo, ed. (2004). Dixon's chapter (pp. 18 and 20) on the Vietnamese Communist Party notes its membership quotas for such groups as trade unions and women. Discussing the social challenges of reform, Clark (p. 101) notes that women are disproportionately affected by economic restructuring in Vietnam. In discussing change in education and health systems in Vietnam, London (p. 135) gives gender disaggregation of lower secondary enrolment rates. In her chapter on health campaigns, Blanc (pp. 154 and 158) mentions the Women's Association. As a result of interviewing young graduates in Hanoi, Phuong An Nguyen (p. 175) notes they do not distinguish between notions of professional and financial success for men and women — a sign of gender equality.

Apart from three books that did not mention women or gender, others often had more than was indicated by their index. A few books stand out as having substantial coverage. They are the single-author books by Weiss (2006) and Kerkvliet (2005), and chapters specifically on women in works edited by Aspinall and Fealy (2003) and by Loh and Khoo (2002). The advantage of an edited volume is that someone with expertise on gender can be invited to contribute (and to make up for other contributors who barely mention women); yet this did not happen in most (eight out of eleven) of the edited works listed here.

The more challenging work of explaining all this now begins. Why do most authors treat gender as irrelevant to Southeast Asian politics? Why do some do better than others in recognizing its importance? What does this tell us about political science as a discipline?

Whether or not gender is noticed depends on the questions that authors are asking. Sometimes the questions point in the direction of gender analysis but authors fail to follow this path. More generally, political scientists pose a narrow range of questions which often exclude gender analysis and reveal the limited view they take of what politics is about. As feminists say, what is frequently required is not just "adding women" to the existing mix, but rethinking paradigms in the light of observing the absence of gender considerations.

QUESTIONS AUTHORS ASK THAT SHOULD INCLUDE GENDER ANALYSIS

Sometimes it is obvious that authors have taken as the focus of their writing a question that directly asks about women, such as "What role have women played in the democratization movement in Indonesia/Malaysia?" Hana Satriyo's and Maznah Mohamad's chapters mentioned above (see Table 4.7) are good examples of such work. As mentioned, this is one way in which an edited text can "mainstream" gender.

Other fruitful questions include those that focus on civil society (Weiss 2006) and on grassroots politics (Kerkvliet 2005). When one looks at non-government organizations and at how rural people behave politically, it is a very gender-blind author who overlooks the existence and activity of women's organizations and female farmers. Whether the author chooses to give much attention to women is another matter, but it is easy to include gender analysis just by asking whether women participated in the phenomena under study and, if so, in what capacity was their activity different from that of men's, and what were its outcomes and why. There are numerous feminist works on such issues.[5]

A number of other authors raise questions which could well be answered in terms of gender, yet they fail to follow through on the analysis. For example, Ziegenhain's (2008) study of the changing role of the Indonesian parliament in the period 1998–2004 evaluates its performance according to three functions: representation, oversight of government, and legislation. Naturally discussion of representation lends itself to gender analysis. As Ziegenhain says (2008, p. 34), "According to the idea of representation, parliaments should represent the opinions of all parts of the population", and adds "Demographic characteristics are one way to analyse the conformity of representatives and constituents." "In theory", he continues, "a national parliament, as the people's representation, should be a mirror of the population of the country. Therefore, an equal gender representation should be targeted as a goal just as poor and working class people should have adequate representation" (pp. 36–37). Understandably, therefore, I looked forward to further analysis of this point in relation to Indonesia's parliament. I was disappointed. In his discussion of the parliament at the end of the New Order regime, representation of women is not mentioned. In his exploration of the parliament's representative function after the 1999 elections, we encounter a major contradiction. Analysing the social profile of the parliament, Ziegenhain (2008, p. 116) acknowledges that "it was not fully representative of the population of the country", among other things because 92 per cent of its members were men. He advances no explanation of why this occurred, nor does he note that this percentage represented a drop in women's representation compared with the last New Order parliament, nor does he mention later legislative efforts to introduce quotas for women to correct the low level of female representation. But this does not stop him from arguing, throughout the rest of the book, that the new parliament "provided the necessary forum for all major social groups, so that none of them felt excluded from the democratic process" (Ziegenhain 2008, p. 180). I am at a loss to explain his reasoning, or his failure to talk to any women's groups about their feelings at seeing women's representation drop. Nor does he ever consider what impact the skewed gender representation may have for the other functions of parliament — oversight and legislation. Ziegenhain (2008) fails to understand the significance of gender analysis for his work.

Similarly, all the studies of elections could quite easily include gender disaggregated data on candidates and members of parliament, yet in the books mentioned that study elections (including not only Ziegenhain's (2008) but also those by Kingsbury (2003), Antlov and Cederroth (2004), Aspinall and Fealy (2003), Gomez (2004), Saw and Kesavapany (2006), McCargo (1998), and Balme and Sidel (2006)), this is almost never done. (A partial exception is Gomez' chapter on the 2004 Malaysian elections in the book edited by Saw and Kesavapany.) Why is it considered unimportant? In any study of democratization, as Ziegenhain (2008) points out, the issue of who is and is not represented must be considered relevant. Studies of Malaysian elections, for instance, would never omit the ethnic aspect of elections yet gender representation remains invisible, despite women being at least half the electorate. Since some of these books point out that in Southeast Asia women are regarded as having relatively high status (e.g. Funston 2001, p. 411), it is fair to ask why they are so under-represented.

Because there is a considerable feminist literature now about women's participation in elections and formal political institutions in Southeast Asia, it should not be difficult for authors to trace the levels of female representation and discuss movements to introduce quotas for women candidates and legislators in different countries.[6]

Another obvious political question to ask, and one posed by some authors, is the issue of who benefits and suffers from policy measures. From a gender perspective, this is a fruitful question, relating to the gender differential in the impact of policies. Yet few authors acknowledge this. In Funston's (2001) book, a key question posed by some authors is: Who has power and who benefits from holding it? Yet there is no mention of the fact that it is men who hold power, or investigation of the consequences of their domination. Case (2002, p. 26) states that the same question is central to his book but his answers focus only on ethnicity, religion and class, never on gender.

Some authors fail to interrogate their data from a gender perspective and thus leave us in the dark as to whether there is significant gender differentiation. Thus, Derichs, in the book edited by Gomez (2004), tells us that she interviewed intellectuals, NGO activists and people in "think tanks" for her chapter on attitudes to reform in Malaysia. However, she gives us no gender breakdown; in fact, her analysis omits gender so we have no way of knowing whether men and women interviewed had significantly different views. A chapter on governance in corporate Malaysia by Yeoh in the book edited by Saw and Kesavapany (2006) makes no mention of whether there is a difference between corporate men and women and a passing reference to "capable corporate men" casts doubt on whether the author even notices that women exist in corporations. In McCargo's (1998) edited book on Vietnam, chapters on the Vietnamese Communist Party tell us nothing about proportions of women in the party or the government. Two chapters in the same book based on interviews in rural situations give no gender analysis of their data.

It should not be too difficult for authors to ask "Where are the women?" in relation to the phenomenon they are studying. This is the easy part of gender mainstreaming: adding the women in. The point of doing so, however, should be not just for the sake of inclusiveness — completing the picture — but also to interrogate what difference it makes to one's analysis to notice women. For example, it may be a matter of identifying how women are differentially affected by policies, or how women's style of leadership may differ from that of men, or whether the structure of women's organizations differs from others.

It is even more adventurous, of course, to ask why women were NOT involved in an event or institution, and if so why not and with what consequences. This would involve recognizing that political phenomena are gendered, something which many authors either ignore or take as given — something apparently too "natural" to mention.[7]

POLITICAL QUESTIONS THAT EXCLUDE GENDER/WOMEN

My point here is that opportunities are missed to observe political differences between men and women in Southeast Asia. Such omissions are easy to spot and not difficult to correct. What is more challenging is when authors pose questions based on a view of politics that seems to allow no space for gender analysis. So, for instance, it is common to find authors concerned to explain regime change (or the lack of it), and in their explanations gender analysis has no obvious place. It is easier to discuss the impact of regimes and regime changes on gender relations, but quite difficult to fit women into causal explanations, if only because every regime is male-dominated. Constructing new categories, such as grouping regimes according to their gender ideologies, may be one way of approaching the question. A deeper analysis of masculinity may also be more relevant than a focus on women. Some acknowledgement that different kinds of masculinity are to be found in different regimes and why would enlarge our appreciation of the relevance of gender analysis in Southeast Asian politics. Unfortunately, as mentioned above, masculinity studies relating to politics are still in their infancy.

Similarly, writers on international relations in Southeast Asia seem convinced that their subject has nothing to do with gender, as witness the chapters on security and foreign policy in *Southeast Asian Affairs 2008* and in the book edited by Balme and Sidel (2006). For the last couple of decades, writing by feminists on international relations has worked hard to bring gender analysis into these areas,[8] but it demands a radical change of paradigms, such as expanding the notion of security beyond military matters. These ideas do not seem to have infiltrated writing on Southeast Asian international relations which continues to pursue the old questions.

Another line of enquiry that remains largely impervious to gender analysis is political economy. It has been interesting over the years to observe the treatment of gender in the books on Southeast Asia edited by Gary Rodan, Kevin Hewison and Richard Robison (2006). Because these authors take a strongly structuralist approach to political economy, focusing on the development of capitalism, they ignore gender. A couple of contributors to their latest edited book (listed in Table 4.1) manage to mention women by discussing the impact of capitalist change on women, but generally these writers have no time for such "social" issues. Women may feature as victims of capitalist policies but because there is no scope here for agency (Case 2002, p. 11), they do not appear as actors. Moreover, since class trumps other categories, gender fades from view. Alternatively, political economy authors frequently take a neo-liberalist perspective in which the market is gender-blind. (Examples are to be found in *Southeast Asian Affairs 2008*.) Much work remains to be done here by feminists, who have been slow to develop new ideas about political economy in general, let alone in Southeast Asia. It is likely to be a long time before dominant political economy paradigms are challenged from a gender perspective in studies of Southeast Asia.[9]

I should hasten to add that I am not arguing that every political question asked should highlight gender analysis. Gender does not have to be centre stage to everything studied. What scholars need to do is to be alert to the gender dimension of what they are studying. Bearing in mind that women make up at least half the population, analysts should ask "Where are the women?" (followed by "Why?" and "What difference does it make to notice them?"). Furthermore, they should ask themselves "Is this concept gendered?" (followed by "How?" and "What difference does it make?"). Seeking answers to such questions may well open up new insights.

Finally, it would help if political scientists would broaden their view of power, which is after all the central concept in their discipline. Some interesting observations have already been made about this in the Southeast Asian context. For example, feminist anthropologists like Suzanne Brenner have for some time been working to show how power in Indonesia is gendered in interesting ways that were not appreciated by analysts like Ben Anderson (Sears 2007, pp. 54-58). Their conceptual narrowness means that political scientists mainly fail to look outside conventional public institutions for the exercise of power.[10] Thus they fail to notice women, who are notoriously under-represented in such institutions. They also ignore other ways in which women are disempowered, some categories of women more so than others of course. It is noticeable that in the works discussed, those who had most to say about gender relations and women were those who looked beyond parties, parliaments and governments to find how power is exercised, experienced and challenged.

WHY THE LACK OF GENDER MAINSTREAMING?

My analysis of mainstream politics books about Southeast Asia shows a very patchy and largely disappointing level of gender mainstreaming. Although edited works offer the opportunity to have at least one chapter addressing gender, most of the compilations I examined give it scant if any attention. As the noted feminist political scientist, Sawer (2004, p. 559) has remarked about Australian politics textbooks, despite the increased willingness of editors to add a feminist chapter:

> there was still a common tendency for material about women or feminist perspectives to be isolated in one specific section or chapter, rather than for gender analysis to be mainstreamed. Men were rarely considered as gendered; gender was a characteristic reserved for women and not considered as part of the overall construction of political life.

The single-authored works on Southeast Asian politics present an uneven picture. Few give any prominence to gender, and some treat it as quite irrelevant, without ever explaining why. There is no correlation between the sex or nationality of the author and interest in gender. However, it is noticeable that most authors employed in political science, international relations and public administration positions display far less knowledge and interest in gender than those from other disciplines like sociology or development studies.[11] It is fortunate that so many from outside the discipline are writing about Southeast Asian politics. Indeed, a recent analysis of the contribution of Southeast Asian studies to political science emphasizes that "some of the most insightful contributions to our understanding of Southeast Asian politics have come from *non*-political scientists" (Kuhonta, Slater and Vu 2008, p. 3).

What is particularly disappointing is that, to judge from these works, most authors writing about Southeast Asian politics do not read the feminist literature in the field. The fact that they have not sought out this literature shows they have not accepted its relevance to their work. It is as if most political scientists categorize books about Southeast Asian women as a specialised field for women's eyes only; men are absolved from consulting such works. (It will be interesting to see whether the rise of masculinity studies breaks this mould.[12]) Somehow writing about more than half the Southeast Asian population is regarded as a marginalized area, whereas we are all expected to read books that are exclusively about men and which never acknowledge that their study is gendered. Under these circumstances, gender cannot be mainstreamed.

I have two recommendations to make. One is to urge political scientists to read feminist works and to expand their views of power and what is political. Focusing on institutions or issues where women are not present is in itself no excuse for neglecting gender, since the obvious problem is to explain why the institution or issue is so male-dominated and what are the consequences of that domination. The failure of scholars to catch on to this point is revealed when women do finally enter their focus area, whether it is government or religious organizations; many scholars continue to write as though women are not present at all.[13]

My second recommendation is for politics teachers and postgraduate supervisors to encourage students to address gender aspects of any question they are studying. Asking "Where are the women?" is a good start, if only because it may lead on to the questions, "Why?" and "What difference does it make?" Only if these questions are asked can gender be mainstreamed in the pursuit of knowledge of Southeast Asian politics. So many political scientists still use a very limited and conservative range of questions in approaching their subject matter, betraying a blinkered view of what politics is about. It reminds me of Paul Valery's definition: "La politique est l'art d'empecher les gens de se meler de ce qui les regarde" (Politics is the art of preventing people from taking part in affairs that properly concern them). In effect, scholars who continue to exclude women and gender issues are implying that they have no legitimate political role, and that politics addresses a very limited range of concerns.

I would conclude that the political science scene is changing only very slowly. This conclusion is supported by those who have made studies of the impact of feminist scholarship on political science in Australia, Canada and the United States.[14] Compared with twenty years ago, there has been some improvement in awareness of gender in mainstream political studies of Southeast Asia, but I am not optimistic that if the level is gauged in another twenty years, the change will be dramatic. The number of feminist political scientists working on Southeast Asia is very small and unlikely to grow rapidly given the inertia of the politics discipline, both inside and outside the region.[15] The vast majority of political science writers mentioned in this chapter are men, although I hasten to add that one should not assume that feminists are to be found exclusively amongst the ranks of women, or even assume that most women writers are feminists. Hope for change seems to come from influences outside the discipline rather than within it.

Notes

1. I shall never forget my feelings of outrage at a Monash seminar delivered in the 1980s by a visiting Indonesian academic. His fieldwork had been on changing political views in a Javanese village. At the end of his talk I asked him what the women had told him about their political views, and he replied that he had not interviewed any women.

2. Clayton, Centre of Southeast Asian Studies, 1991.

3. In a recent book about Southeast Asian studies, Laurie Sears notes that the field has been slow to absorb "concerns with race, ethnicity, and gender... It was not until the 1990s that books about gender and feminist theory began to appear within Southeast Asian studies..." ("Postcolonial Identities, Feminist Criticism, and Southeast Asian Studies", in *Knowing Southeast Asian Subjects*, edited by Laurie J. Sears (Seattle: University of Washington Press, 2007).

4. Alfred W. McCoy, "Same Banana: Hazing and Honor in the Philippine Military Academy", *Journal of Asian Studies* 54, no. 3 (1995): 694, quoted in Sears 2007, p. 58.

5. Examples include Cecilia Ng, Maznah Mohamad, and tan beng hui, *Feminism and the Women's Movement in Malaysia: An Unsung (R)evolution* (New York: Routledge, 2006); M. Oey-Gardiner and C. Bianpoen, eds., *Indonesian Women: The Journey Continues* (Canberra: Australia National University Press, 2000); Kathryn Robinson and Sharon Bessell, eds., *Women in Indonesia: Gender, Equity and Development* (Singapore: Institute of Southeast Asian Studies, 2002); and Susan Blackburn, *Women and the State in Modern Indonesia* (Cambridge: Cambridge University Press, 2004).

6. Examples of such literature are Wil Burghoorn, Kazuki Iwanaga, Cecilia Milwertz, and Qi Wang, eds., *Gender Politics in Asia: Women Manoeuvering within Dominant Gender Orders* (Copenhagen: Nordic Institute of Asian Studies Press, 2008); and Kazuki Iwanaga, ed., *Women's Political Participation and Representation in Asia: Obstacles and Challenges* (Copenhagen: Nordic Institute of Asian Studies Press, 2008). The subject is also taken up in Ng, Mohamad, and

tan (2006) and Blackburn (2004). The International Institute for Democratic and Electoral Assistance has championed the cause of women's representation with publications like *Memperkuat Partisipasi Politik Perempuan di Indonesia* (Stockholm: International Institute for Democratic and Electoral Assistance, 2003).

7. An excellent early example of a work that focuses on omission of gender in policy-making is Jomo, Kwame S., and Tan Pek Leng, eds., *Missing Women: Development Planning in Asia and the Pacific* (Kuala Lumpur: Asian and Pacific Development Centre, 1985).

8. The works of Cynthia Enloe, V. Spike Peterson, and Christine Sylvester would be relevant here.

9. A pioneering example of applying feminist ideas to political economy in Malaysia is Cecilia Ng, ed., *Positioning Women in Malaysia: Class and Gender in an Industrialising State* (Houndmills: Macmillan, 1998).

10. Although not especially concerned about gender analysis, Carlo Bonura also laments that Southeast Asian politics has been characterized by a lack of "recognition of political power as functioning outside established political institutions" ("Political Science, the Anxiety of Interdisciplinary Engagement, and Southeast Asian Studies", in ibid, p. 322).

11. Sawer (2004, p. 560) notes about Australia: "With rare exceptions, male political scientists do not seem to have followed their colleagues in sociology or cultural studies in developing an interest in gender." As an example from the works examined in this paper, it is noticeable that the contributors to *Southeast Asian Affairs 2008* are almost all employed in international relations and political science departments — and the volume makes no mention at all of women or gender.

12. Given the failure of Women's Studies centres to make inroads into political science, I am not hopeful of the success of masculinity studies within Gender Studies centres. Such centres have become ghettoised in many universities.

13. For instance, the book by Robert Hefner on Muslims and democratization in Indonesia unaccountably says nothing about women as participants in debates within Islam, *Civil Islam: Muslims and Democratization in Indonesia* (Princeton: Princeton University Press, 2000).

14. See Sawer (2004), pp. 553–66; J. Arscott and M. Tremblay, "Il reste encore des travaux a faire: Feminism and political science in Canada and Quebec", *Canadian Journal of Political Science* 32, no. 1 (1999): 125–51; and Sue Tolleson-Rinehart and Susan J. Carroll, "'Far from Ideal': The Gender Politics of Political Science", *American Political Science Review* 100, no. 4 (2006): 507–13.

15. I have no figures on men and women teaching or researching on Southeast Asian politics, but studies for Australia and the United States show that women still constitute a minority of political science staff and are concentrated in the lower ranks (Sawer 2004, pp. 563–64; and Tolleson-Rinehart and Carroll 2006, p. 511). Predictably, the study of the contribution of Southeast Asian studies to

political science, edited by Kuhonta, Slater and Vu (2008) contains no indication that the field has given rise to new insights in relation to gender.

References

Antlov, Hans and Sven Cederroth, eds. *Elections in Indonesia: The New Order and Beyond.* London: RoutledgeCurzon, 2004.

Arscott, J. and M. Tremblay. "Il reste encoure des travaux a faire: Feminism and political science in Canada and Quebec". *Canadian Journal of Political Science* 32, no. 1 (1999): 125–61.

Aspinall, Edward and Greg Fealy, eds. *Local Power and Politics in Indonesia: Decentralisation and Democratisation.* Singapore: Institute of Southeast Asian Studies, 2003.

Balme, Stephanie and Mark Sidel, eds. *Vietnam's New Order.* London: PalgraveMacmillan, 2006.

Blackburn, Susan. *Women and the State in Modern Indonesia.* Cambridge: Cambridge University Press, 2004.

Burghoorn, Wil, Kazuki Iwanaga, Cecilia Milwertz, and Qi Wang, eds. *Gender Politics in Asia: Women Manoeuvring within Dominant Gender Orders.* Copenhagen: Nordic Institute of Asian Studies Press, 2008.

Case, William. *Politics in Southeast Asia: Democracy or Less.* London: Zed Books, 2002.

Funston, John. *Government and Politics in Southeast Asia.* London: Zed Books, 2001.

Gomez, Edmund Terence, ed. *The State of Malaysia: Ethnicity, Equity and Reform.* London: RoutledgeCurzon, 2004.

Hefner, Robert. *Civil Islam: Muslims and Democratization in Indonesia.* Princeton: Princeton University Press, 2000.

International Institute for Democratic and Electoral Assistance. *Memperkuat Partisipasi Politik Perempuan di Indonesia.* Stockholm: International IDEA, 2003.

Iwanaga, Kazuki, ed. *Women's Political Participation and Representation in Asia: Obstacles and Challenges.* Copenhagen: Nordic Institute of Asian Studies Press, 2008.

Jomo, Kwame S. and Tan Pek Leng, eds. *Missing Women: Development Planning in Asia and the Pacific.* Kuala Lumpur: Asian and Pacific Development Centre, 1985.

Kerkvliet, Benedict J. Tria. *The Power of Everyday Politics: How Vietnamese Peasants Transformed National Policy.* Ithaca: Cornell University Press, 2005.

Kingsbury, Damien. *Politics of Indonesia.* Melbourne: Oxford University Press, 2005.

Kingsbury, Damien and Harry Aveling, eds. *Autonomy and Disintegration in Indonesia.* London: RoutledgeCurzon, 2003.

Kuhonta, Erik M., Dan Slater, and Tuong Vu, eds. *Southeast Asian in Political Science.* Stanford: Stanford University Press, 2008.

Loh Kok Wah, Francis and Khoo Boo Teik, eds. *Democracy in Malaysia: Discourses and Practices.* Richmond: Curzon, 2002.

McCargo, Duncan, ed. *Rethinking Vietnam*. London: RoutledgeCurzon, 2004.

Ng, Cecilia, ed. *Positioning Women in Malaysia: Class and Gender in an Industrialising State*. Houndmills: Macmillan, 1998.

Ng, Cecilia, Maznah Mohamad, and tan beng hui. *Feminism and the Women's Movement in Malaysia: An Unsung (R)evolution*. New York: Routledge, 2006.

Oey-Gardiner, Mayling and Carla Bianpoen, eds. *Indonesian Women: The Journey Continues*. Canberra: Australian National University Press, 2000.

Robinson, Kathryn and Sharon Bessell, eds. *Women in Indonesia: Gender, Equity and Development*. Singapore: Institute of Southeast Asian Studies, 2002.

Rodan, Gary, Kevin Hewison, and Richard Robison, eds. *The Political Economy of Southeast Asia*. Melbourne: Oxford University Press, 2006.

Saw Swee-Hock and K. Kesavapany, eds. *Malaysia: Recent Trends and Challenges*. Singapore: Institute of Southeast Asian Studies, 2006.

Sawer, Marian. "The Impact of Feminist Scholarship on Australian Political Science". *Australian Journal of Political Science* 39, no. 3 (2004): 553–66.

Sears, Laurie J., ed. *Knowing Southeast Asian Subjects*. Seattle: University of Washington Press, 2007.

Southeast Asian Affairs 2008. Singapore: Institute of Southeast Asian Studies, 2008.

Stivens, Maila, ed. *Why Gender Matters in Southeast Asian Politics*. Clayton: Centre of Southeast Asian Studies, 1991.

Tolleson-Rinehart, S. and S.J. Carroll. "Far from Ideal: The Gender Politics of Political Science". *American Political Science Review* 100, no. 4 (2006): 507–13.

Weiss, Meredith. *Protest and Possibilities: Civil Society and Coalitions for Political Change in Malaysia*. Stanford: Stanford University Press, 2006.

Ziegenhain, Patrick. *The Indonesian Parliament and Democratization*. Singapore: Institute of Southeast Asian Studies, 2008.

5

GENDER MAINSTREAMING IN HEALTH: MAINSTREAM OR "OFF-STREAM"?

Rashidah Shuib

INTRODUCTION

The evolution from the WID (Women in Development) approach to the GAD (Gender and Development) approach brought the political language of the feminist discourse to the forefront of discussions in the international development agenda. It was argued that putting on the gender lens would result in a clearer, more realistic view of the conditions and the position of women and men in society. In the area of health, the GAD approach helped to widen the perspective on development, as health issues became included as integral to a country's development. Locating the issues within the gender framework was seen as a way of finding answers as to why gender inequality and inequity exists. The adoption of the word "gender" which replaced "women" is seen as a step forward in gender mainstreaming. Moser and Moser (2005, p. 11) in their paper reviewing the success and limitations of gender mainstreaming since Beijing have evaluated the progress on gender mainstreaming in three stages:

*   adopting the terminology of gender equality and gender mainstreaming;

- putting gender mainstreaming policies into place; and,
- implementing gender mainstreaming.

These stages will be assessed in this chapter in an effort to map the various components of gender mainstreaming policy in health specifically in the contexts of Cambodia, Malaysia, the Philippines, and Vietnam.

The 'buy-in' to the idea that tackling gender inequality is critical to development led governments across the world to accept gender mainstreaming as a strategy to achieve gender equality and the empowerment of women. International organizations, donors, United Nations (UN) agencies and non-government organizations (NGOs) have assisted many countries with financial and technical assistance and capacity building to facilitate structural changes. Gender specialists and gender focal points were "located within a centralized team, as well as 'embedded' in decentralized departmental and regional offices" (Moser and Moser 2005, p. 14). Manuals, toolkits and checklists were also developed. Given the range of initiatives to ensure gender mainstreaming, one would have imagined that the literature would be rich with success stories and best practices. A cursory look at the literature on gender mainstreaming, however, shows that it is peppered with words such as "defanged", "gender fade away", and "gender evaporation", giving the impression that gender mainstreaming as a mechanism in achieving gender equality is "weak", has "evaporated", and "lacks bite" or that the implementation of this concept is mere "tokenism". The question then is to ask whether these words describe the reality or are they mere weapons of the critique of gender mainstreaming as argued by some (Moser and Moser 2005; Ravindran and Kelkar-Khambete 2007; North 2008; Kalyati 2008).

This chapter aims to visit gender mainstreaming in health issues in a select number of countries in Southeast Asia in order to assess whether gender mainstreaming as envisioned by the feminist movement is still palpable and "on-course" or whether it has gone "off-course", as has been the fate of some policies and strategies adopted by governments. To offer a deeper understanding of the issues in hand, the chapter begins by retracing briefly the historical context to gender mainstreaming and the philosophy which underlies the term. The chapter also examines the term "gender mainstreaming" which has been argued by some to be problematic.

The chapter is divided into several sections. The main section of this chapter examines gender mainstreaming against the backdrop of the geo-political and socio-economic scenario in Southeast Asia, especially sexual and reproductive health and rights issues which are rife with controversies, and the nature of the implementation of the concept of gender mainstreaming in the countries of Cambodia, Malaysia, the Philippines, and Vietnam. It must be noted that these countries were chosen for two reasons: (a) the availability of literature on gender mainstreaming in health in the Southeast Asian region; and, (b) my experiences of having been involved in capacity-building efforts [for health practitioners] in two of the four countries. Lastly, the chapter presents my reflections and observations of capacity-building efforts and strategies adopted in gender mainstreaming based on my own involvement in gender and rights training on health issues in Cambodia and Malaysia. The chapter concludes by arguing that gender mainstreaming in health, as it has been implemented, has basically gone "off-course". As a strategy which originally aims to challenge gender inequality, it has now been stripped of its original motives and underlying philosophy. In a nutshell, the political intent underlying gender mainstreaming has disappeared. As a result, feminist politics aimed at ensuring gender equality in development efforts has, in turn, become de-politicized while the technicalities of gender mainstreaming instead have come to be retained. The outcome at best is a patchwork of gender mainstreaming strategies which are lacking in cohesiveness and clarity of direction.

GENDER MAINSTREAMING: RETRACING HISTORY

The term "mainstream" first appeared in the education scene in the 1970s, reflecting calls to place disabled children together with non-disabled children in the same classroom (Charlesworth 2005). The idea was to ensure that disabled children would not be isolated and marginalized. The concept emphasized bringing children perceived to be "not so normal" to be part of the mainstream education system; in sum, it is an attempt to normalize the school system.

The phrase "mainstreaming gender" in the feminist discourse has a different history. As early as the 1980s, the word "mainstream" found its way into the vocabulary of the women's movement. The Third World Conference on Women in 1985 called for "...special measures designed to enhance women's autonomy, bringing women into the mainstream of the development process... (United Nations 1986, para. 111) and further emphasized that "...effective participation of women in development should be integrated in the formulation and implementation of mainstream programs and projects..." (United Nations 1986, para. 114). It was here, according to Correa (1994), that the debate on population began to heat up. The language of the neo-liberals and Christian fundamentalists argued on the "neutrality" of population issues and called for free-market forces as the fuel for economic growth. On the contrary, the feminists argued that family institutions, as part of the population dynamics, are not and cannot be neutral, pointing to the fact that families are products of social constructions as much as gender, which is also socially constructed.

This debate continued to gain momentum at the 1994 International Conference on Population and Development (ICPD) in Cairo and the 1995 Fourth World Conference on Women in Beijing. By this time, there was more clarity on the need to adopt the gender perspective in order to move towards a gender equal society, while at the same time, the Vatican and the Islamic fundamentalists took a more visible conservative stance on issues of abortion, reproduction, sexuality and adolescent health. It was in this emotionally-charged environment that the term "gender mainstreaming" became incorporated into the language of the documents of the two conferences (Charlesworth 2005; Correa 1994) and accepted by governments as the key strategy for achieving gender equality and women's empowerment (North 2008). Gender mainstreaming, once accepted, was theoretically meant to address unequal power relations in society by transforming institutions and structures which maintain gender inequalities. One can argue that to stay "on-course", this strategy has to remain true to its feminist political ideology and its philosophic principles of human rights and justice.

GENDER MAINSTREAMING:
DEFINITION AND CONCEPTUAL CONFUSIONS

Some critiques of gender mainstreaming have argued that one of the problems with the term is the lack of conceptual clarity. This problem was highlighted at meetings reviewing the progress five years and ten years after ICPD and the Beijing Conference (Licuanan 2005; Hannan 2005). I, however, see it not as an issue of conceptual clarity; rather it is an overloaded and complex term with multiple dimensions and meanings. In an attempt to obtain conceptual clarity, the Economic and Social Council (ECOSOC) of the United Nations provided the following definition in 1997 (Division for the Advancement of Women 1997):

> Mainstreaming a gender perspective is the process of assessing the implications for women and men of any planned action, including legislation, policies and programmes, in all areas and at all levels. It is a strategy for making women's as well as men's concerns and experiences

an integral dimension of the design, implementation, monitoring and evaluation policies and programmes in all political, economic and societal spheres so that women and men benefit equally and inequality is not perpetuated. The ultimate goal is to achieve gender equality.

Since the United Nations (UN) decided to implement gender main-streaming throughout the UN system, ECOSOC also identified additional guidelines for the UN to follow (Report of the Economic and Social Council for the Year 1997, supra note 21, at 24, cited in Charlesworth 2005, p. 5):

Issues identified across all areas of activity should be defined in such a manner that gender differences can be diagnosed — that is, an assumption of gender-neutrality should not be made.

Responsibility for translating gender mainstreaming into practice is system-wide and rests at the highest levels. Accountability for outcomes needs to be monitored constantly.

Gender mainstreaming also requires that every effort be made to broaden women's participation at all levels of decision-making. Gender mainstreaming must be institutionalized through concrete steps, mechanisms and processes in all parts of the United Nations system.

Gender mainstreaming does not replace the need for targeted, women-specific policies and programmes or positive legislation, nor does it substitute for gender units or focal points.

Clear political will and the allocation of adequate and, if need be, additional human and financial resources for gender mainstreaming from all available funding sources are important for the successful translation of the concept into practice.

Looking at the definition, it is easy to detect the multidimensional aspects and complex tasks which have to be undertaken in order to operationalize the concept. Gender mainstreaming is first and foremost an ideology which challenges the existing patriarchal societies. But clearly, it is also a process, a strategy which requires technical knowledge and skills to operationalize on the ground. Gender analysis becomes critical and the availability of sex and gender disaggregated data is a necessity for gender analysis to be conducted. In addition, gender mainstreaming has been perceived to be too broad and the goal too idealistic and difficult to measure. It takes a long time to see visible social changes on the ground. It has also been perceived to be too narrow and myopic because it neglects the intersectionality of gender, that is, how gender intersects with various social and cultural factors such as race and class to contribute to oppression and privileges in society. But more specifically in the case of health, the concept of the intersectionality of gender refers to the various ways gender intersects with the social determinants of health.

GENDER MAINSTREAMING: THE CONTEXTUAL LANDSCAPE

The other dimension which this chapter intends to highlight is the need to understand gender mainstreaming in Southeast Asia against the backdrop of the region's geopolitical and economic scenario. Health, particularly sexual and reproductive health, is a complex subject and when played out within the context of Southeast Asia, this complexity is further amplified by rapid globalization, migration within the region, and the changing economic landscape, leading to enormous challenges in gender mainstreaming.

The Geopolitical and Socio-Economic Scenario

Southeast Asia is a region of differences, rich in diversity. At the Conference on the Future Prospects of the East Asian Economy and Its Geographical Risk on 23 February 2004, Teo (2004) identified 'three waves of fundamental changes and transformation and shifting geo-politics and geo-economics' impacting on the region. These are the Wave of Liberalization or Globalization, the Wave of the 1997–98 Asian Crisis, and the third, the Wave of the 12 October 2003 Bali bombing and the SARs epidemic of that same year. These three waves were significant influences on the region's economy and trade relations. The latest Wave of the Global Financial Crisis will further add to areas of internal conflict and economic development. Yet Villegas (2008) predicts that based on the World Economic Outlook by the International Monetary Fund (IMF), Southeast Asia will stay resilient economically, although GDPs in the region are predicted to decline. Table 5.1 shows a forecast that Indonesia and Vietnam will maintain the highest GDP while Singapore will be the lowest in 2009. China's economy is forecasted to score the highest GDP at 9.3, India second with a GDP of 6.9, while the economic superpower of Japan will slip into a deep recession. As this region is faced by these crises, it is hard not to conclude that the application of gender mainstreaming in development has not and will not suffer. It is clear that financial commitment to development will slow down during economic downturns, particularly since meeting

TABLE 5.1
GDP Growth Rates, 2007–09*

Southeast Asia	2007	2008F	2009F
Indonesia	6.3	6.1	5.5
Malaysia	6.3	5.8	4.8
Philippines	7.2	4.4	3.8
Singapore	7.7	3.6	3.5
Thailand	4.8	4.7	4.5
Vietnam	8.5	6.3	5.5
Northeast Asia			
China	11.9	9.7	9.3
Hong Kong	6.4	4.1	3.5
Korea, Republic of	5.0	4.1	3.5
Taiwan	5.7	3.8	2.5
Other			
India	9.3	7.9	6.9

Note: *Only data from 2007–09 are included in this chapter.
Source: Bernado M. Villegas, "Global Recession and Its Impact on the Asian Economy", in *World Economic Outlook*, International Monetary Fund, October 2008 (Washington, D.C.: International Monetary Fund (IMF), 2008), p. 65.

practical needs are priority by governments even among the Southeast Asian economies predicted to continue to grow.

Sexual and Reproductive Health and Rights: An Unending Site of Contestations

As alluded to in the earlier part of this chapter, gender mainstreaming in health issues has its beginnings prior to the ICPD 1994 in Cairo. But the 1994 ICPD represents the watershed in the women's movement in health. The language of population control became intertwined with the language of individual choice and rights. For the first time sexual and reproductive health and rights took centre stage. Reproductive health was given a new meaning; one that was seen to empower women to take control of their own bodies. In a nutshell, women's empowerment in the area of health was seen to be fundamental to development. Correa (1994, p. 9) puts it succinctly when she writes that:

...transforming the population field in order to effectively apply the reproductive and rights framework is conditioned upon a virtual revolution in prevailing gender systems and development models. Along with their commitment to human rights, women's bodily integrity and reproductive self-determination, reproduction related policies must be conceived and implemented as part of a renewed human development paradigm that fosters democratic institutions and, most importantly, equitable economic policies.

IMPLEMENTATION OF GENDER MAINSTREAMING: CAMBODIA, MALAYSIA, THE PHILIPPINES AND VIETNAM

By 2009, fifteen years would have passed since the United Nations conference in Cairo where the women's health movement saw triumph (even if momentarily) in putting the controversial sexual and reproductive health and rights issues at the centre of the population debate. This section attempts to assess the success (or failure) of gender mainstreaming in selected Southeast Asian countries.

As alluded to earlier in this chapter, some voices criticized gender mainstreaming as a failed strategy. But there are voices which are more cautious on drawing such a conclusion. Rao Gupta and Mehra (2006) cautioned that it is still too early to pass such a judgement; instead they argue that success in gender mainstreaming is likely to be progressive rather than resulting in a total transformation. Some of these obvious changes could be in the form of "...staffing, policies, developing indicators, and training of all staff, which are often interpreted as preconditions or precursors to interventions at the operational level" (Rao Gupta and Mehra 2006, p. 2). Using Moser and Moser's (2005, p. 13) framework of how international development institutions have mainstreamed gender, nine components were outlined for analysis (as shown in Table 5.2):

- dual strategy of gender mainstreaming plus targeted, specific actions for gender equality which should be reflected in country policies;
- gender analysis of healthcare needs;
- combined responsibilities comprising of staff who should be trained as well as gender experts or specialists;
- gender training to build capacity;
- support to women's decision-making and empowerment;
- monitoring and evaluation using gender sensitive indicators;
- working with other organizations;

TABLE 5.2
Components and Associated Activities of Gender Mainstreaming Policy in Health

Components	Activities	Malaysia	Philippines	Vietnam	Cambodia
Dual strategy of gender mainstreaming and targeted gender equality	Mainstreaming gender into policies, projects and programmes (all stages of cycles)		X	X (Gender Equality Law)	X
	Actions targeting gender equality	X (HIV/AIDS)	X	X (abortion, violence against women (VAW))	X
Gender analysis	Sex disaggregated data + gender informaton	X (HIV/AIDS)	X	X (very early stage)	X
	Analysis at all programme stages				
	Gender-sensitive budget analysis	X (pilot)	X (5 per cent dedicated to gender)		
Internal responsibility	Responsibilities shared between all staff				
	Gender specialist/Gender focal point	X	X	X	X (GMAG)

TABLE 5.2 (*Cont'd*)

Components	Activities	Malaysia	Philippines	Vietnam	Cambodia
Gender training	Understanding and implementation of gender policy for staff		X		X
	Staff gender sensitization	X	X	X	X
	Staff gender training skills	X	X	X	X
	Manual, tool kits	X	X	X	X
Support for women's decision-making and empowerment	Strengthening women's organizations through capacity building and training				
	Support women's participation in decision-making empowerment				
	Working with men for gender equality				
Monitoring and evaluation	Effective system and tools for monitoring and evaluation		X		
	Gender-sensitive indicators		X	X	

TABLE 5.2 (*Cont'd*)

Components	Activities	Malaysia	Philippines	Vietnam	Cambodia
Work with other organizations	Strengthening gender equality in work with other government agencies, NGOs and private sectors	X (but initiatives by NGOs and Ministry of Women)			
	Capacity building of civil society		X	X	X
	Support to national women's machinery		X	X	X
Budgets	Allocation for staff to carry out gender policy	X (for gender training)	X	X	Funders
Knowledge resources	Publication of knowledge based on best practices		X		X
	Networks				
	Online databases				

- gender budgets; and,
- knowledge resources.

Table 5.2 gives a summary of the extent gender has been mainstreamed in the activities of the selected four countries in the Southeast Asian region.

GENDER INFRASTRUCTURE AND THE LANGUAGE OF GENDER EQUALITY AND GENDER MAINSTREAMING

In all the four countries, the burden of advancing gender equality and the empowerment of women are entrusted to the government national machineries dealing with women's issues. In Malaysia, it is the Ministry of Women, Family and Community Development (MWFCD); in the Philippines, it is the National Commission on the Role of Filipino Women; the National Committee for the Advancement of Women (NCFAW) acts as the Focal Point on Gender Policy in Vietnam; while in Cambodia, the job is given to the Ministry of Women Affairs (MOWA). It is apt to conclude that the machineries to further advance gender issues in these countries have been established. It is, therefore, expected of these bodies to convince other ministries on the need to integrate gender issues. This can be tricky and the success depends very much on the kind of relationships established across the ministries and how those ministries view the women machineries. Nevertheless, in all the four countries, there are Gender Focal Points being placed in the Ministry of Health. The main role of these Focal Points is to champion the integration of gender within the Ministry's work. An interesting mechanism is the establishment of the Gender Mainstreaming Action Group (GMAG) in the Ministry of Health, Cambodia whose members come from various departments within the Ministry and are appointed by the Minister for Health. The strength in this approach is that there is a team to work on gender mainstreaming rather than leaving it to an individual.

Moser and Moser (2005) argued that the first step forward would be to adopt the language of gender equality and gender mainstreaming. Looking at the documents produced by the Ministries of Health in Cambodia, Vietnam and the Philippines, it is clear that the language of gender is well integrated. In the case of Malaysia, the term 'equity' is embodied in the Ministry's mission but nothing is mentioned about gender. In contrast, the language seems to be visible in the Malaysia's National Strategic Plan on HIV/AIDS 2006–2010 which mentions that "Gender inequalities must be addressed in the response" (Ministry of Health Malaysia, p. 10) as one of its core guiding principles. However, there is no mention on how this principle will be operationalized.

PUTTING IN PLACE A GENDER MAINSTREAMING POLICY

Unfortunately it is difficult to conclude that the four countries have successfully put in place a gender mainstreaming policy in health with all the nine key components as identified by Moser and Moser (2005). Vietnam has passed a Gender Equality Law on 29 November 2006 which was implemented in 2007. But how this law is brought into effect in the health sector is anyone's guess. Vietnam has also passed the Law on Domestic Violence Prevention and Control but this is all still very new and, thus, difficult to assess. What is certain is that there is little data on domestic violence against women, rape and sexual violence, implying that much more needs to be done to tackle these issues. Notably the new National Strategy for the Advancement of Women in Vietnam by 2010 does include five key objectives with discrete targets to achieve by 2010. One of these objectives is "equal rights for women in health care" (NCFAW 2004). In the case of the Philippines, there is a clearer policy on gender mainstreaming particularly with respect to budgeting. Since 1995, the Philippine Government implemented a policy that five per cent of all government agency budgets should be spent on gender and development projects and activities (Yao 2006; ESCAP 2004). The Philippines has also decided to have gender equality measures in the form of Core Gender and Development (GAD) indicators, and Harmonized GAD Guidelines for Project, Development, Implementation, Monitoring and Evaluation. The country has also put in place the requirements for Gender Focal Points and has also established Gender Resource Centres and Gender Resource Kits. Priority areas which have been earmarked are reproductive health and violence against women (health) and micro-enterprise (economic development). Cambodia has also developed its health policy and programme for action but the objectives and the indicators mentioned do not reflect gender equality and gender mainstreaming. A case in point is that the indicators are basically conventional indicators of mortality and morbidity. There is also no evidence of gender analysis of health situations being done using sex disaggregated data (Kingdom of Cambodia 2002). In the case of Malaysia, gender is not reflected in its current health policy. As alluded to in the previous section, the only document that is closest to integrating gender is the Malaysia National Strategic Plan on HIV/AIDS 2006–10 which states clearly that gender equality is one of its guiding principles. On the other hand, the Ministry of Health does support capacity-building programmes in gender mainstreaming by committing a specific fund for that purpose, thus enabling a training programme to be conducted yearly for its doctors and paramedics since 2005.

IMPLEMENTING GENDER MAINSTREAMING

Critiques have lamented that there is a big chasm between the language used and the intentions announced in the implementation of the concept of gender mainstreaming. A review done by Asia-Pacific Resource and Research Centre for Women (ARROW) of findings from country monitoring studies in Cambodia, China, India, Indonesia, Malaysia, Nepal, Philippines and Pakistan in 2004 revealed that despite having new reproductive health and population policies, these policies have no clear reproductive rights and women's rights framework. In other words, programmes may have shifted beyond family planning and population control to comprehensive reproductive health programmes but these programmes are not necessarily guided by the reproductive rights framework, as embodied in the ICPD Platform for Action 1994. In Malaysia, for example, compulsory pre-marital HIV/AIDS testing for Muslim couples clearly violates human rights and reproductive rights. In the Philippines, the Catholic Church has strongly influenced the country's push for the natural family planning method. In many countries, the provision of contraceptives is only for married couples. The right to sexual education for adolescents is not respected. Gender analysis is not done. This situation is a far cry from what was found in the women's health policies and programmes prior to the gender mainstreaming movement. According to Ravindran and Kelkar-Khambete (2007), gender analysis was not only fundamental to women's health policies but more important, it was empowering at the same time. In their article, several enabling conditions for gender mainstreaming were identified (Ravindran and Kelkar-Khambete 2007, p. 18):

- presence of international, national and regional mandates for relevant activities to be initiated;
- presence of political will;
- establishment of legal and constitutional frameworks that support gender equality;
- availability of resources; and,
- presence of strong women's health and/or human rights, and movement and a culture of active civil society participation.

All of the four countries in this review have ratified international documents such as the Convention on the Elimination of All Forms of Discrimination Against Women (CEDAW) as well as the Cairo Programme for Action, besides some other international consensus. Thus, these enabling environments are fulfilled. The pressure to report to CEDAW, for example, has helped to push for specific actions to ensure that gender is mainstreamed in certain areas. The weakness, however, is that countries like Malaysia have not signed on to the Optional Protocol, thus, limiting citizens from exercising their rights when violations of certain CEDAW clauses occur. Political will is a questionable enabling factor in these countries as well. The Philippines, for example, has the political will to implement progressive reproductive health programmes only to withdraw them when the government gives in to pressures from the Catholic Church. As a result, only natural family planning methods are advocated. Abortion is also not allowed. The presence of strong women's health and civil society movements is a plus but then again, it does not guarantee that gender mainstreaming will actually take place when indeed gender equality is the goal. Again the Philippines represents an example of a country with strong people's power, but fares poorly in terms of ensuring universal access to contraceptives and safe abortion.

But the author maintains that the crunching factor is the availability of resources to be galvanized for gender mainstreaming activities. A poor country like Cambodia, which is heavily donor dependent, may not be the best place to start full gender mainstreaming activities when the government is concerned with meeting basic daily needs. In addition, capacity is also an issue when gender team members have to work in more than one job to make ends meet. My experience of conducting gender and rights training among health managers in Cambodia was that the participants were not ready to adopt the concepts related to gender equality because 'doing gender work' for many of them was seen to be over and above their duties.

One area that all four countries seemed to have undertaken is capacity building and gender training for various groups. The subject matter covered ranges from conceptual understanding of basic gender concepts to gender indicators and how to conduct a gender analysis and undertake a gender budget. Perhaps training is an easier realm to be involved in because numbers can indicate success or failure. In short, the biggest problem in Cambodia, Malaysia, the Philippines and Vietnam is the poor implementation of gender mainstreaming coupled with gender analysis. Because gender analysis is absent, this means that no questions have been asked of existing power relations and, therefore, it is expected that transformation is likely not to have taken place.

CAPACITY BUILDING AS A GENDER MAINSTREAMING STRATEGY: GENDER AND RIGHTS TRAINING IN HEALTH — A PERSONAL REFLECTION

Capacity building with a focus on training seems to be the most common strategy taken by many countries in the region to mainstream gender, including the four countries selected for analysis in this chapter. In this section, I share my experiences and observations based on the gender training sessions I had facilitated in Malaysia and Cambodia. The course in Cambodia was a consultancy project of ARROW to meet the request of the GMAG from the Ministry of Health Cambodia. In the following section, I assess whether the gender training conducted actually led to gender mainstreaming.

Without a doubt, capacity building is important to any organization, particularly when new concepts need to be understood, norms and values have to be changed, and knowledge and skills are crucial for transformation to take place. Gender mainstreaming in health requires institutional mainstreaming of the lead agency which, in this case, refers to the Ministry of Health. It entails, according to Hannan (2003), that workers must be able to handle gender mainstreaming as part and parcel of their professional competence.

But what do we understand by capacity building? What dimensions and characteristics should it imbue? According to the United Nations Development Programme (UNDP), capacity building is the creation of an enabling environment with appropriate policy and legal frameworks, institutional development, including community participation (of women, in particular), human resources development and strengthening of managerial systems (UNDP 1991). The other characteristics of effective capacity building are that it should be long-term, and constitute a continuous process involving all stakeholders. This implies planned and sustained programmes. UNDP (accessed 5 May 2007) has also identified core dimensions of capacity building which are listed below:

- appropriate knowledge and skills with an understanding of gender equality and ability to use tools and information. This is to be expected of all staff;
- strategic management which provides leadership in policy implementation and ability to create and nurture an environment supportive of gender mainstreaming;
- effective networks and linkages, linking units within and with external organizations;

- enabling policy and institutional environments which support gender equality interventions; and,
- supportive economic, social and political environments consistent and supportive of gender mainstreaming.

MALAYSIA:
GENDER AND RIGHTS TRAINING IN MATERNAL AND REPRODUCTIVE HEALTH

This five-and-a-half-day course was an adapted version of the three-week WHO's training curriculum for health programme managers: a course on "Transforming Health Care Systems: Gender and Rights in Reproductive Health". This programme has been implemented once yearly since 2005 with full funding from the Ministry of Health coordinated by the National Institute of Health (NIH). Participants are medical doctors including obstetrics and gynaecologists, family physicians and public health doctors, medical assistants, and senior nurses chosen by the Ministry of Health. The final selection of participants is made by State health departments. The NIH emphasizes the need to choose participants who are in leadership positions to moot changes. The content-packed course covers: conceptual clarifications on basic gender terms, the social determinants of health and poverty, gender indicators, the importance of engendering policy, and introducing change. Participants are encouraged to implement a gender-related intervention at their workplace.

Strengths

- Ownership of the programme by the Ministry of Health even though the introduction of the course was externally produced.
- Other facilitators/resource persons are also from the Ministry, thereby ensuring sustainability.
- Seen as valuable because of the link with WHO's course.
- Credibility is important. Facilitator was perceived as a 'gender expert' because of her membership on the Gender Advisory Panel, Department of Reproductive Health and Research, WHO Geneva for six years, besides being trained in the original module.
- Sustained effort because of adequate and committed funding from the Ministry of Health.

Weaknesses

- The NIH has no control on the selection of participants or on whether the States are obliged to send in their staff as participants.
- Weak on gender analysis because of time constraints.
- Follow-up training such as on gender analysis skills and engendering research is needed.
- Lack of post-training monitoring and support to participants on their planned projects.
- Change of norms and values on gender equality among participants is highly suspect.
- Obvious lack of sex disaggregated data for discussions.

CAMBODIA: GENDER AND RIGHTS IN MATERNAL AND REPRODUCTIVE HEALTH FOR HEALTH MANAGERS

Like the Malaysian version, this course, taught in Phnom Penh, was partly adapted from the WHO original Gender and Rights course but with new materials added on to meet the local needs of the health managers. The participants of the course included some senior health managers and members of the GMAG. GMAG is the group entrusted to advance gender issues within the Ministry of Health and in the healthcare system. GMAG identified training as the immediate work need and saw their task of training health managers at the provincial level to be important. For that purpose, the course was further modified with local cases after consultation with the GMAG. The course with the provincial health managers, held in Sieam Reap, was facilitated by the GMAG with the assistance of facilitators, although the first phase of training the trainers among the GMAG was done in Phnom Penh.

Strengths

- The course was developed to allow for local contents/cases to be included. It was felt that the GMAG would be in the position to introduce those changes.
- The course was to meet the needs of the GMAG members who felt that they needed health-specific gender training. The one that they received from the Ministry of Women's Affairs was too general.

- The strategy of training the GMAG to be trainers would result in local capacity building.

Weaknesses

- Sustainability is questionable because funding for the training came from the United Nations Population Fund (UNFPA). In a country like Cambodia which relies heavily on donor funds and is beset with poverty, this begs this question of whether gender mainstreaming should be seriously adopted in health development efforts or whether a country should reach a minimal (at whatever level this is pegged) level of economic stability before embarking on gender mainstreaming.
- Lack of local sex-disaggregated data for discussions.
- No time for gender analysis.
- Some topics could be too difficult for some participants who came from different backgrounds with little grounding in social issues. It should also be noted that highly qualified workers are badly lacking since many highly qualified professionals died during the country's civil war. Cambodia is one country struggling to recover from years of internal strife.
- Like the Malaysian case, actual changes in norms, values and beliefs in gender equality among the participants are highly suspect.

CONCLUSION

This chapter has attempted to show that gender mainstreaming in health has not taken place. Majority of the countries claim that they see the importance in gender equality and the need for gender mainstreaming but in actuality they are reluctant to question the existing system or the power relations within the system, preferring to retain the status quo or opting to do it "our way" and not imitating the West. This implies an unwillingness to accept the ideology of gender equality and the framework of rights and justice.

On balance, an assessment of health policies in the four countries in Southeast Asia reveals that whatever gender mainstreaming that has been done is merely superficial and patchy. The process has become de-politicized and delinked from the actual aim of social transformation and social justice; instead the emphasis has been on application of techniques and tools. The fact that the link between health and rights is unclear and fragile has added another dimension of complication. There is an urgent need to bring gender mainstreaming back "on-course" by tapping into the potential convergence between the women's right approach and the gender and development approach (O'Neill 2004). The tool that is available to achieve this end is CEDAW which must be aligned with gender mainstreaming so that the human rights discourse once again becomes the political language of gender mainstreaming (Ruiz-Austria 2007). CEDAW, adopted in 1981, is the key international legal instrument on women's rights, addressing issues in the private as well as the public sphere. When governments ratify the treaty, they are obliged to report to the CEDAW Committee on their obligations. Non-Government Organizations (NGOs) provide pressure by providing their "shadow" or alternative country reports. As alluded to earlier in the chapter, gender mainstreaming is a strategy towards achieving gender equality which requires an ideological shift on the part of governments. CEDAW not only acts as a monitoring mechanism but it also sets a global normative human rights framework against which gender mainstreaming achievements can be benchmarked. For gender mainstreaming not to be a mere technicality, it must be informed by CEDAW which is basically the rights framework.

References

Asia-Pacific Resource and Research Centre for Women (ARROW). *ICPD Ten Years On: Monitoring on Sexual and Reproductive Health and Rights in Asia*. Kuala Lumpur: ARROW, 2004.

Charlesworth, Hilary. "Not Waving but Drowning: Gender Mainstreaming and Human Rights in the United Nations". *Harvard Human Rights* 18 (2005): 1–18 <http://www.law.harvard.edu/students/org/hrj/iss18/charlesworth.pdf> (accessed 29 November 2008).

Correa, Sonia. *Population and Reproductive Rights: Feminists Perspectives from the South*. London: Zed Books, 1994.

Division of the Advancement of Women, United Nations Department of Economic and Social Affairs. "Gender Mainstreaming". Extract from Report of the Economic and Social Council A/52/3, 18 September 1997 <http://www.un.org/womenwatch/daw/csw/GMS.PDF> (accessed 25 November 2008).

Economic and Social Commission for Asia and the Pacific (ESCAP). "Malaysia's National Population and Family Development Board Resource Centre", 2009 <http://www.unescap.org/esid/psis/population/popin/profiles/mys.nsp> (accessed 7 January 2009).

———. "Selective Examples of Good Initiatives of Gender Mainstreaming in Development. Technical Papers". High-Level Intergovernmental Meeting to Review Regional Implementation of the Beijing Platform for Action and Its Regional and Global Outcomes, Bangkok, 7–10 September 2004.

Hannan, Carolyn. "Gender Mainstreaming: A Key Strategy for Promoting Gender Equality at National Level". Prepared for a panel — Moving Beijing Forward: Strategies and Approaches for Creating an Enabling Environment, at the UNESCAP High-Level Intergovernmental Meeting to Review Regional Implementation of the Beijing Platform for Action and Its Regional and Global Outcomes, 7–10 September 2004.

————. "Overview on Gender Mainstreaming". In *Putting Gender Mainstreaming into Practice*. New York: United Nations Economic and Social Commission for Asia and the Pacific, 2003.

Kalyati, E. "Avoiding Fade Away: Gender and Budgets in Malawi". *EQUALS* Issue 20 (April 2008): 4.

Kingdom of Cambodia. "Ministry of Health: Health Sector Strategic Plan 2003-2007 Framework for Annual Operational Plans". Cambodia: Ministry of Health, 2002.

Licuanan, P.B. "Beijing + 10 Meets Millenium + 5". Outline/Speaking Notes, 2005 <http://www.adb.org/Documents/Events/2005/Beijing-Meets-Millenium/presentation-licuanan.pdf> (accessed 30 November 2008).

Ministry of Health Malaysia. "Malaysia National Strategic Plan on HIV/AIDS 2006–10". Putrajaya: Ministry of Health Malaysia, 2006.

Moser, C. and Annalise Moser. "Gender Mainstreaming Since Beijing: A Review of Success and Limitations in International Institutions". *Gender and Development*, 13, no. 2 (2005): 11–22.

National Committee for the Advancement of Women (NCFAW). "Vietnam Progress Report on the Implementation of Women in APEC", 2004/SOMIII/GFPN/024. Paper presented at the Gender Focal Point Network, Chile, 26–27 September 2004.

North, A. "From Checklists to Transformation: Gender Mainstreaming Since Beijing". *EQUALS* Issue 20 (April 2008): 1–3.

O'Neill, P. "Rethinking Gender Mainstreaming (or, Did We Ditch Women When We Ditched WID?) — A Personal View". *Development Bulletin*, no. 64 (2004): 45–48.

Rao Gupta, Geeta and Rekha Mehra. "Gender Mainstreaming: Making It Happen", February 2006 <http://siteresources.worldbank.org/INTGENDER/Resources/MehraGuptaGenderMainstreamingMakingItHappen.pdf> (accessed 1 November 2008).

Ravindran, T.K.S. and A. Kelkar-Khambete. "Gender Mainstreaming in Health Policies, Programmes and Within the Health Sector Institutions". Background paper prepared for the Women and Gender Equity Knowledge Network of the WHO Commission on Social Determinants of Health. Geneva: World Health Organization, 2007.

Ruiz-Austria, Carolina S. "Alignment of Gender Mainstreaming Efforts Under CEDAW". Paper presented at the Regional Conference on Gender Mainstreaming in Kuala Lumpur, Malaysia, 7–8 May 2007.

Teo, Chu Cheow. "Geo-political Risks in Southeast Asia". Paper presented at the Conference on Future Prospects of East Asia Economy and Its Geopolitical Risks, 23 February 2004 <http://www.mof.go.jp/english/others/ots022n.pdf> (accessed 29 November 2008).

United Nations (UN). "Report of the World Conference to Review and Appraise the Achievements of the United Nations Decade for Women: Equality, Development and Peace", Nairobi, 15–26 July 1985 <http://www.un.org/womenwatch/confer/nfls/Nairobi1985report.txt> (accessed 1 December 2008).

United Nations Development Programme (UNDP). "Capacity-Building", 1991 <http://sdnp.undp.org/gender/capacity/review tables.html> (accessed 5 May 2007).

Villegas, B.M. "Global Recession and Its Impact on the Asian Economy", 2008 <http://www.slideshare.net/guest5e256f8/global-recession-and-its-impact-on-the-asian-economy-presentation> (accessed 29 November 2008).

Yao, Myrna T. "Gains in Gender Mainstreaming: The Philippine Experience". Paper presented by the Chairperson, National Commission of the Role of Filipino Women at the Gathering of National Women's Machines in East Asia organized by the Government of Japan, 2006 <http://www.gender.go.jp/eastasia/2006-07-07.pdf> (accessed 2 December 2008).

6

POLITICIZATION OF ISLAM IN INDONESIA AND MALAYSIA: WOMEN'S RIGHTS AND INTER-RELIGIOUS RELATIONS

Maznah Mohamad

INTRODUCTION

Global attention on what goes on in Muslim-majority countries has been keen since 11 September 2001. The perception is that civil and human rights are jeopardized when radical Islam is in control. Gender equality is also one of the more contentious elements of debates whenever Islam is forcefully asserted in society. In this chapter, I will try to give a balanced assessment on the development of Islam and the question of gender rights in the two Muslim-majority countries of Southeast Asia. The chapter will focus on some controversial developments with regard to the issuance of new regulations, laws and religious opinions (*fatwa*) that impact women and society in Indonesia and Malaysia. The general trend has been mixed since the number of legislations and policies which have tried to redress gender inequalities have increased, while at the same time legislative curbs on women's behaviour and freedom of expression have also equally multiplied. This chapter ends by suggesting that the institution of democracy needs to be kept alive so that a vibrant and civil atmosphere can be sustained for the exchange of dissenting views and opinions. Any resolution to the conflicts must also be worked out in ways that are democratic, consensual and legally binding.

Since this chapter seeks to compare two countries, Indonesia and Malaysia, it is also necessary to be cognizant of the historical and political similarities and differences between the two nations. While both countries project an assertive Islamic politics, it is also important to realize that there are pluralities and diversities within their societies that must be explicated in order to understand the dynamics of an evolving and, therefore, changeable state of Islamization in each country.

I will begin by giving a brief introduction to the background of Islamization in each country. The section brings out some of the differences in the process, in that in Malaysia it was a centralization exercise which strengthened Islamization in state and society and led to the observed trends discussed in this chapter. This is in contrast to Indonesia in which it was the post-Soeharto decentralization period which saw the rise of the more active contestation among civil society elements there. Hence, in Malaysia it was centralization, while in Indonesia it was decentralization which stimulated some of the contentions around gender and Islam.

Figure 6.1 shows that Indonesia is the largest Muslim-majority country in Southeast Asia with about 88 per cent or 189 million of its population being Muslim. Brunei's Muslim population is 67 per cent although in absolute numbers, this amounts to less than half a million people professing the Islamic faith. Malaysia's Muslim population is about 14 million or

FIGURE 6.1
Muslim in Southeast Asia

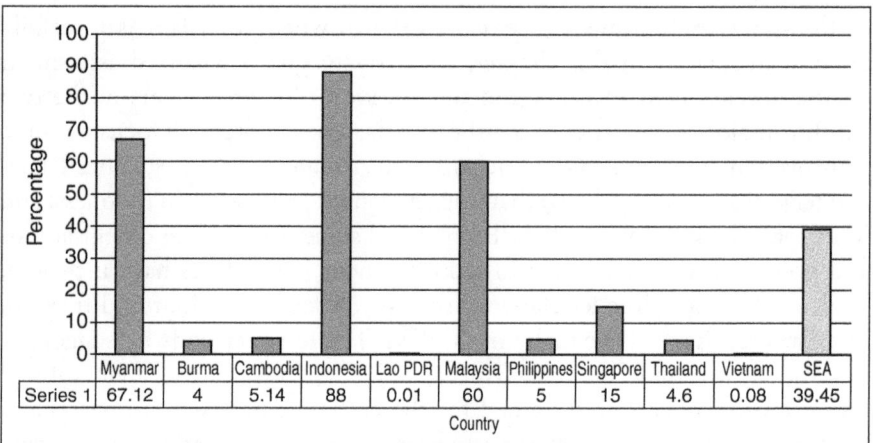

	Myanmar	Burma	Cambodia	Indonesia	Lao PDR	Malaysia	Philippines	Singapore	Thailand	Vietnam	SEA
Series 1	67.12	4	5.14	88	0.01	60	5	15	4.6	0.08	39.45

Source: Adapted from Fealy and Hooker (2006), p. 7.

60 per cent of the total population of the country. Hence in terms of actual population, there is a wide difference between the size of Indonesia's Muslim population as compared to the rest of the Muslim populace in Southeast Asia. Nevertheless both Indonesia and Malaysia have been equally prominent in terms of the role that Islam has played in their politics of democratization and gender justice.

ISLAM AND THE INDONESIAN STATE

In Indonesia, the confrontation over Islam and the state sees two sides. One side represents Islamists who want the *Syariah* to be constitutionally recognized and Islamic laws comprehensively adopted. The other group, broadly known as the secular or sometimes *abangan*, wants the state to be neutral in religious matters since an Islamic state will discriminate against minorities and non-Muslims. These two groups first clashed when the constitution was being drawn up during the eve of Independence in 1945. A compromise was needed to reconcile the demands of the Islamists with the Secularists. The subcommittee tasked to resolve this issue agreed to a "constitutional preamble known as the Jakarta Charter containing a seven-word clause that obliged Muslims to implement Islamic law" (Fealy and Hooker, p. 47). However, this was rejected by a new committee that met on 18 August, the day after Independence was declared. Later on under Soeharto's New Order, debate on Islamizing the State was outlawed. This issue resurfaced after Soeharto's resignation but was again rejected by the Indonesian Parliament. But in 1946, the government did set up the Ministry of Religious Affairs to oversee the Islamic courts, and family matters involving marriage, divorce, inheritance and Islamic charitable foundations. The religious courts in Indonesia now come under the Supreme court (Fealy and Hooker 2006).

In the case of Aceh, the government of Indonesia gave the region its 'special region' status in order to pacify the civil war. Article 4 (1) of Law 44/1999 permitted the implementation of the *Syariah* law. Under the post-Soeharto democratization movement, the governance of Aceh was further decentralized through Law 18/2001 giving autonomy to the region and with it the re-establishment of *Syariah* courts in Aceh (UNDP (nd), p. 47).

Another aspect of the decentralization process is through the passing of the Local Government Act 2004 (*Undang-Undang Nomor 32 Tahun 2004*) which essentially gives authority to local governments to legislate on some areas that are specific to the needs of the region. In some regions, these by-laws are known as the *Perda Syariah* as *Syariah*-related laws have been adopted under this new legislative provision.

In Indonesia, Islamic and non-Islamic courts were already established from colonial times. However, no *Syariah* laws were specifically enacted. It was only in 1974 that a common marriage law was passed, in an attempt to unify the diverse cultural and religious marriage laws which were still in existence in modern Indonesia. However, it was the post-Soeharto decentralization politics which provided the widest opportunity for Islamization to take off. Today, the Aceh *Syariah* laws which were enacted with the granting of an autonomous status for Aceh can be said to be more draconian than the Malaysian variety, especially in terms of the punishments meted out for certain offences.

ISLAM AND THE MALAYSIAN STATE

In Malaysia, what was later constituted as *Syariah* was actually a British legacy which infused this body of laws with elements of Islam, native customs and the sovereign Malay kingship. Nevertheless, Islamic laws went through a systematization process whereby the jurisdiction was limited to family, personal status codes and matters of inheritance. As the Federation of Malaysia has thirteen states and a federal territory, fourteen separate Islamic enactments were passed by each state legislature.[1] This early post-colonial process of entrenching Islamic laws into the body politic of the nation-state project took place between 1952 and 1974.

From 1984 onwards, when the Federal Territory Administration of Islamic Laws Enactment was passed, the centralization and augmentation of the *Syariah* system began to take on a swifter pace. The 1984 Enactment was crucial as it paved the way for the establishment of a more uniform set of Islamic laws on a national level. Under this provision, the office of the Mufti and the Islamic Religious Council would be separated from the *Syariah* Court administration itself. The *Syariah* court system was then expanded into a three-tier system — The *Syariah* Subordinate Court, the *Syariah* High Court and the *Syariah* Appeals Court. With this single new legislation, the Islamic state bureaucracy experienced a multifold expansion almost overnight. By 1991, all thirteen states and a federal territory within the Federation had established the three-tier *Syariah* court system.

Previously *Syariah* was largely confined to family laws, which include laws on inheritance, charitable trusts, and matrimonial and Islamic offences. Provisions for *Syariah* criminal offences were not included as a separate enactment but were part of the administration of Islamic Laws Amendment 1952 in Selangor for example, with some seventeen sections on this (Siti 2006, p. 205). By the 1980s, attention was given towards the introduction of laws on Islamic criminal offences. For example, fifty-two sections on criminal matters were included in the Muslim Religious and Malay Customs Enactment of 1982 of Pahang. In Terengganu, one hundred sections were inserted in the 1986 Enactment of the Administration of Islamic Affairs. Kelantan was the first state to enact the full-fledged *Syariah* Criminal Offences law in 1983. It also passed an enactment on whipping as a punishment (*Kaedah-Kaedah Hukuman Sebat*) in 1987 to distinguish whipping under Islam from that used in the penal code.

As a whole, the centralization of Islam occurred most extensively under the Mahathir Government, starting from about the mid-1980s onwards. The central body which coordinates implementation of Islam in the country today is JAKIM (*Jabatan Kemajuan Islam Malaysia*), or the Department for Islamic Development in Malaysia. Thus, state-driven Islam was the basis for an extensive Islamization project. Today 'bureaucratic Islam' or the elements of state Islamic apparatus may even be more powerful than political parties or even the traditional rulers in influencing Islamization in the country.

WHY ISLAMIZATION THROUGH LAW-MAKING AND LEGALISM?

When Islamic laws gained the focus of attention in the project for Islamic reformation, they had to compete with civil laws which were already in place. It can be said that law-making within the *Syariah* framework must look for areas untouched by civil laws. Normally what is left is the personal and private, or the realm of family litigations and rights. Another area is morality which could never really be legislated in an absolute way within the civil system. Morals as a subject and area of control is where religious laws can find their grip, to the extent that it is morality rather than justice which will begin to consume *Syariah* law-makers in their mission to expand the hold of religion over society (Gadis 2008). In this atmosphere, civil rights and citizenship (for the Muslim) are curbed by invoking the "naturalness" of belonging to a religious faith and authority rather than to the sovereign national state.

INDONESIA'S UNIFYING MARRIAGE LAW

One of the earliest issues of gender contention is the controversial passing of the Marriage Law, Act No. 1 of 1974 which was adopted as a guideline by judges in the Secular Courts and applicable to both Muslim and non-Muslim citizens. In order to reconcile the role of the *Syariah* in the governance of Muslims, the three-volume Compilation of Islamic Law (CIL) is used to guide Islamic courts when using the common Marriage Law (Cammack 1998,

p. 68). However, the CIL is not an enactment but a code implemented through Presidential Instruction in 1991. Thus the CIL can be said to be Indonesia's only model of an Islamic Law covering the areas of marriage law (*nikah*), inheritance law (*waris*) and charitable foundation law (*waqaf*).

Nevertheless, women's rights proponents object to the CIL as it is said to be based on a male-biased interpretation of Islamic law, such as on issues of:

- *nusyuz* (disobedience of wife),
- rights and responsibilities of spouses,
- earning of livelihoods,
- polygamy,
- inter-religious marriage,
- *iddah* (the waiting period),
- *ihdad* (the mourning period), and
- adopted and extra-marital children.

Under the CIL, inter-religious marriage is also prohibited. Furthermore, according to Dr Musdah Mulia who heads the Gender Unit of the Ministry of Religious Affairs, there are several contradictory provisions (in the form of laws, policies, international treaties, *fatwa* and opinions) which either allow or prohibit Muslim-non-Muslim marriages. Such a situation has caused both a confusion of citizen's rights and the denial of marital unions between couples of differing faiths. She said that this had led to the increase of unregistered marriages. Her opinion states that marriage is a right and the government's duty is merely to record and register rather than come in-between citizens' happiness and choice — "Marriage recording is the government's obligation and the right of every citizen. The government is obliged to record marriage contract entered into by any one of its citizens with whatever religion or faith, and is also obligated to record inter-religious marriage concluded by its citizens because the state's duty and obligation are to have the marriage filed or recorded not to have it legitimized."[2]

Another controversy which has erupted around religion and to a certain extent gender is the Pornography Law (*UU Pornografi*), which was passed by the Indonesian Parliament on 30 October 2008. This piece of legislation basically bans pornography but the definition as to what this means is made too broad and all-encompassing. Such a regulation transgresses private spaces and includes questionable definitions of indecent dressing, behaviour and actions. On top of it all, the law provides for the existence of 'vigilantes' or ordinary citizens to take on the role of a moral police force in the enforcement of the law.[3]

DECENTRALIZATION OF INDONESIA:
SYARIAH IN ACEH

Indonesia's political decentralization allows for by-laws to be established at the regional or provincial levels. These laws are called the *Peraturan Daerah* or *Perda*. In 2001, a law was passed giving special autonomy for Aceh which permits the establishment of the *Syariah* courts and the implementation of Islamic laws. This paved the way for the introduction of laws beyond family laws, such as laws to prohibit specific offences deemed 'criminal' under an Islamic system. There are now specific Islamic criminal offences, not found in national laws under the *Qanun Syariah* Aceh (Syariah Code of Aceh) (UNDP (nd), p. 48), namely:

a. *Qanun* 11/2002 on *aqidah* (correct belief), *ibadah* (ritual worship) and *Syi'ar* Islam (promoting greatness of Islam)
b. *Qanun* 12/2003 on *khamar* (liquor)
c. *Qanun* 13/2003 on *Maisir* (gambling)
d. *Qanun* 14/2003 on *khalwat* (illicit relations)[4]

The *Qanun Provinsi Nanggroe Aceh Darussalam, Nomor 11 Tahun 2002 Tentang Pelaksanaan Syariat Islam, Pasal 13* stipulates the following:

(1) Setiap orang Islam wajib berbusana Islami.
(2) Pimpinan instansi pemerintah, lembaga pendidikan, badan usaha dan atau institusi masyarakat wajib membudayakan busana Islami di lingkungannya.

In essence, the above law makes it mandatory that an Islamic dress code be followed by everyone within the province and all national leadership and the public sector must encourage Islamic dressing within their midst.

Yet another law under the *Qanun Provinsi Nanggroe Aceh Darussalam, 14 Tahun 2003, Tentang Khalwat (Mesum)* stipulates that:

Setiap orang yang melanggar ketentuan sebagaimana dimaksud dalam pasal 4, diancam dengan 'uqubat ta'zir berupa dicambuk paling tinggi 9 (sembilan) kali, paling rendah 3 (tiga) kali dan/atau denda paling banyak Rp.10.000.000, — (sepuluh juta rupiah), paling sedikit Rp2.500.000, — (dua juta lima ratus ribu rupiah).

What is significant in the above law is that there is a severe punishment for unmarried couples caught in an intimate act or being in close proximity. The punishment entails whipping — the minimum being three lashes and the maximum nine.

One of the main concerns of laws such as the above is that the jurisdiction of the laws is not explicitly spelled out. This means that even a non-Muslim may be subjected to the laws above (UNDP (nd), p. 48).

Another concern is that there is an institution being set up to monitor *Syariah* conduct and compliance to *Syariah* law within Acehnese society. The *Wilayatul Hisbah* (WH) is one such institution which is authorized to provide "moral guidance" to Muslims. Officials and members under its set-up have extensive powers at the village and provincial levels. But there have been reports that the WH has been overzealous in its role of moral policing to the extent that actions of their members could potentially violate Constitutional Law and human rights. Some of the punishments meted out arbitrarily by the WH have included, "cutting off the hair of women caught without a *jilbab* (head scarf); slapping of women; unlawful detention; and, cutting the pants of women that are considered by WH members to fit too tightly, thus shaming women publicly" (UNDP (nd), p. 91).

INTER-RELIGIOUS FAMILY LITIGATIONS IN MALAYSIA

The period of the mid-2000s was especially filled with a great number of controversial inter-religious family litigations. Many taken-for-granted institutions for civic guarantees were tested, such as the Federal Constitution, the *Syariah* Laws, the civil courts, and the executive in affording citizens their rights to civil liberty, freedom of religion, and rights to state protection. Some of the cases involved Muslim-non-Muslim marriages, others involved the jurisdictional powers of the *Syariah* court as opposed to the civil courts, and yet others involved rights to conversions.

As summed up, the then Opposition leader Lim Kit Siang, in referring to the predicaments of Raimah and Marimuthu (see note below) — "It is sad and tragic that a happy couple and united family with seven children as a result of 21 years of marriage should be broken up by religious factors when family unity and love should be the paramount concern of all religions" (Kuek Ser Kuang Keng 2007). Below are examples of this dire situation of forbidden inter-religious marriages.

The Raimah and Marimuthu Case

Raimah and Marimuthu were married based on Hindu rites in 1976. They had seven children. In April 2007, seven officers from the Selangor Religious Office (JAIS) visited their home and told Marimuthu that his wife of twenty-one years was a Muslim and that she and her children, aged between four and twelve must be placed in a rehabilitation centre. A religious scholar had also approached Marimuthu to convert to Islam or threatened to charge him for *khalwat* (close proximity) with Raimah. In May 2007, the Selangor Religious Authority forced Raimah to separate from her husband and sent her to a rehabilitation centre. To save the family, Raimah reluctantly gave up custody of her children to Marimuthu and was then not allowed to live together with her husband and children.

The Reevathi Case

Reevathi was born to Indian Muslim parents who gave her a Muslim name, Siti Fatimah. She claimed to have been raised as a Hindu by her grandmother and changed her name in 2001. In 2004, she married her Hindu husband, Suresh Veerappan according to Hindu rites although the marriage is not legally registered as Suresh would have to convert to Islam first. In January 2007, Reevathi was detained by the Islamic Religious Department of Malacca and sent to a religious rehabilitation centre. They also seized her fifteen-month-old daughter from her husband and handed her over to Reevathi's Muslim mother. Her detention period of a hundred days was further extended by eighty days in April 2007.

The Magendran and Najeera Case

This case involved a twenty-five-year-old Hindu man Magendran Sabapathy and his Muslim wife Najeera Farvinli Mohamed Jalali who had been married for a year. They went through a Hindu wedding ceremony. In late April 2007, five officers from the Selangor Religious Department told him that his Hindu marriage was void and warned that he would be charged for unlawful cohabitation under Muslim law (*khalwat*). He relented and was separated from his wife who was then believed to be under JAIS's custody. Currently, a notice of motion has been sent to the Shah Alam High Court for Magendran to be reunited with his wife.

POLYGAMY IN MALAYSIA

In Malaysia, laws on polygamy have now made it easier for Muslim males to take on four wives. Ever since Muslim family laws were promulgated in the country, the right of a Muslim man to marry more than one wife up to a maximum of four has always been recognized. However, certain conditions were applied to this entitlement. During the early years, the Muslim enactments in certain states required that the man acquire the written permission of the *Kadi* (Islamic judge) in order to do so. This is still in contradiction of certain *adat* (customary) laws in which the rule was monogamy. In the state of Negri Sembilan, for example, where the matrilineal system pervades, a Malay could not marry a second wife without obtaining the permission of the ruler and the consent of the first wife (Ahmad 1965, p. 187).

Over the years, amendments to Muslim family laws have inserted more specific requirements such as for a formal application to be made to the court. During such hearings, all the existing wives will be called to appear before the court after which a judgment will be made as to whether the marriage is "appropriate and necessary". In some states, a written permission from the *kadi* must be obtained by the man before he can enter into a polygamous marriage. Failure to comply with these conditions is an offence, liable to a fine or imprisonment. There were in fact landmark judgments that favoured women. The conditions to be fulfilled for polygamy were stringent. In the case of *Aishah bte Abdul Rauf vs Wan Mohd Yusof bin Wan Othman*, the wife's appeal to overturn the *Kadi*'s decision to allow for the husband to take on a second wife was granted by the Selangor State Appeal Committee, even though the husband was someone of material means. The rules were strict at that time and in favour of women (Horowitz 1994).

However, starting from the mid-1990s, these rules have been gradually relaxed. In the state of Selangor, a clause requiring the written permission of existing wives to consent to the polygamy was removed in 1996. Women's groups protested but this did not succeed in reversing the situation.

In 2005, there were further new rules which tried to lessen the economic burdens of husbands in their quest to propagate and maintain multiple families. In that year, amidst vociferous opposition from women's groups, Parliament passed the Islamic Family Law (Federal Territories) (Amendment) Bill. These amendments have discriminatory effects upon women. Among the amendments made were those which included the rights of husbands to claim part of their existing wives' assets or joint property upon his new marriage. Under this amendment, wives of polygamous husbands are forced to choose either to apply for order of maintenance or to apply for order of division on joint property. They could only choose one or the other and not both as sources for maintenance. This has no basis in Islamic law as the conventional version had always made it mandatory for a husband alone to maintain his wives. Another amendment gives an additional right to a husband to apply for a dissolution of marriage under judicial order (known as *fasakh* divorce in Islamic law). Before this amendment was made, *fasakh* was solely a right granted to women. There are twelve grounds of divorce under this clause, which includes desertion, violence and non-maintenance. However, the granting of divorce by judicial decree to a husband is superfluous as he already has the unilateral right to divorce without reason. The only reason why a man would apply for divorce under *fasakh* would be to avoid paying compensation to the divorced wife. The other discriminatory amendment under the new regulation was to allow for a husband to obtain a court injunction to prevent the disposition of property by a wife or former wife in order to protect the husband's claims on the property in the event of a legal contest.[5] Women's groups called these moves blatant and unabashed as they seemed designed to make it easier for Muslim males to practise polygamy while freeing them from some of the stringent conditions of taking on economic responsibility towards the welfare of co-wives and multiple families.

FURTHER EXPLANATION ON THE ISLAMIC FAMILY LAW (FEDERAL TERRITORIES) (AMENDMENT) 2005[6]

The controversial amendments to the Islamic Family Law (Federal Territories) were passed by the Malaysian Parliament on 26 September 2005. I detail the nature and implication of the amendments below.

(i)   Section 23 (9), stipulates that "…every court that grants the permission or orders a marriage to be registered under this section shall have the power on the application by any to the marriage…to order the division between the parties of the marriage of any assets by them during the marriage by their joint efforts or the sale of such assets and the division of the proceeds of the sale." By this it is meant that a husband has a right to claim a share of his existing wife's property (*harta sepencarian*) upon his polygamous marriage.

(ii) Sections 23 (3) and 23 (4)(a): Through these sections, the application for polygamy is made easier for men. Under the previous law, section 23 provided that the proposed polygamous marriage must be proven to be "just and necessary". With the amendment, the key phrase is now changed to "just or necessary" implying that husbands need only show that the marriage is "necessary" and need not show that he will also be "just" in the marriage.

(iii) Section 23 (9)(a) essentially forces a wife to choose maintenance or division of *harta sepencarian* upon a husband's polygamous marriage. According to some opinions, this has no basis in Islamic law as it is a mandatory obligation for a husband to maintain his wife.

FATWA AND CONTROL OVER SEXUALITY

An aspect that has emerged among Muslims today is the power of religious authorities to pronounce a *fatwa* or a religious opinion on an issue or an action that is in need of clarification and a ruling from an Islamic point of view. *Fatwa* are the theological and legal reasonings given by a *mufti* or the *ulama* to explain, clarify and eventually pronounce a deed sinful or acceptable. In Malaysia, under the *Syariah* Criminal Offences laws, one cannot defy, disobey or dispute a *fatwa*. Furthermore, once a *fatwa* is pronounced, it is then gazetted to become law without the issue being tabled for debate in parliament or the state legislative body. This is quite different from Indonesia wherein a *fatwa* can have enormous moral clout but it may not necessarily be translated into enforceable laws.

In October and November 2008, two controversial *fatwa* were issued by the Malaysian National Fatwa Council. The first *fatwa* was on 'tomboys' or prohibition against women who are dressed like men. The second *fatwa* was on the banning of yoga among Muslims. The first *fatwa* makes it illegal for women to appear and/or dress like men, as the idea is to criminalize lesbianism. The other prohibits Muslims from practising yoga, following the argument that it is a form of worship involving chanting and meditation and may go against the Islamic *aqidah* (belief).

Women's groups were quite vociferous in condemning the above prohibitions because largely the rulings were seen as rather careless and arbitrary in nature. For example, there is no clear definition of what 'dressing like a man' entails, as wearing trousers and shirts may even be construed to be so. Besides, the suggestion that 'dressing like a man' is a sign that someone is necessarily lesbian is far-fetched and even absurd. The *fatwa* on yoga was considered excessive and misplaced as yoga is conventionally understood (and practised) as a form of exercise rather than a faith. Here again, the suggestion that doing yoga may lead to one's faith in Islam being shaken is also far-fetched and absurd. Although the trend of trying to control women's bodies and sexuality is not new among Islamic authority, the new *fatwa* has certainly brought about unprecedented outrage among a broad section of the Malaysian population because of its "extremism". As opined by Masjaliza Hamzah, the Programme Manager of Sisters in Islam: "The ongoing debate and controversy surrounding the recent *fatwas* on tomboys and yoga have brought to fore opinions and trends that are unprecedented in the history of Muslim societies and jurisprudence, and alarming in multi-faith and democratic Malaysia."[7]

CONTESTATIONS, DEBATES AND CHALLENGES

Despite the above onslaught of regulations and control, women in the two countries have not been totally subjugated by the developments, but have also provided challenges to the system. In Indonesia, women activists have introduced a Counter Legal Draft (CLD) to provide an alternative to the government's CIL. This was drafted by The Gender Mainstreaming Team of the Ministry of Religious Affairs in collaboration with a committee of Islamic legal scholars and women activists in Indonesia. Officially the CLD was made public in November 2004. This is a model draft of Islamic Family Law which is an alternative draft to the current Compilation of Islamic Law. The draft tries to put forward another version of Islamic Family Law for contemporary situations, particularly on gender equality and for recognizing inter-religious marriage. The CLD is said to be "constructed on the premise that the realization of the Qur'anic vision of the family can be achieved only if the values of humanity, equality and freedom are reflected in all aspects of the family law".[8] Indonesia also has a National Commission on Violence Against Women (KOMNAS-Perempuan) set up under a Presidential Decree.

In Malaysia, contestations, debates and challenges to some of the laws which discriminate women can be seen in the proposal for the "Repeal of the Amendments to Islamic Law in Malaysia". This is a campaign led by the group, Sisters in Islam together with the Joint Action Group of Women Against Violence (JAGWAV). There has also been opposition to the *fatwa* against 'tomboys' and yoga which came in quite swiftly after the announcement of the *fatwa*. Besides women's groups, the Sultans or the traditional Malay rulers have come out to oppose the implementation of the *fatwa*.

In Malaysia, the Islamization drive had also initiated women's demands for fairness and justice within the *Syariah* system. The movement has also pressured the government to institute a system which can protect women against recalcitrant husbands and fathers. For example, the *Syariah* Judicial Department has now set up a special division called the Family Support Authority to enforce *Syariah* court decisions on family-related and divorce cases. By this it is meant that experienced officers will be based in all *Syariah* courts to help in the enforcement of judgments, particularly cases involving maintenance claims and matrimonial compensations. The government is also looking into the setting up of an Islamic Family Foundation to provide aid to families experiencing difficulties when going through a divorce (Mazwin 2008; Hamidah 2008).

POLITICS BEHIND ISLAMIZATION

What are the politics behind such a fervent move to push for Islamic rules and regulations to such an extent that civil and gender rights may be transgressed? In Aceh, the *Syariah* implementation came as part of the autonomy deal and a bargain in the post-tsunami peace process. In the rest of Indonesia, the post-Soeharto decentralization led to the burst of diverse religious opinions and practices. Islam is seen to be pluralized and with it the assertion of distinct cultural practices and norms. The *UU Pornografi* also underscores the kind of alliance politics that the various stakeholders are trying to foster. It was said that the passing of this law was a move by President Susilo Bambang Yudhoyono to win over some Muslim allies in order to counter the force led by Megawati and her party the PDI-P.[9]

In Malaysia, the centralization of Islam was a strategy that was used by UMNO to contain all other Islamic contenders and maintain its hegemony and legitimacy over Malay-Muslims. The expansion of the *Syariah* system saw the rise of a new class of bureaucratic Islamists, which initiated the reforms behind the Family Law, for example. The *Fatwa* Councils also exercised its control by cutting down competition from other sources of Islamic authority.

THE FUTURE

In future, it will be difficult to combat some of the above forces once Islam becomes more and more entrenched through laws. Unlike secular laws where one is allowed to debate, reject and repeal any provision since nothing is sacrosanct or cast in stone, it would be different with the *Syariah*. *Syariah* law is considered divine and, therefore, unchangeable, even if the original passing of *Syariah* legislations may have actually been debated and adopted through modern parliamentary procedures. Debate must, therefore, continue to be promoted. Furthermore, the participation by non-Muslims in these exchanges should also be seen as an essential essence of democracy because all laws, even if it is said to apply (theoretically) to only Muslims, will ultimately, in practice, 'spill over' and affect every citizen in the nation-state.

DEMOCRACY AS A PILLAR OF ENGAGEMENT

In conclusion, I would like to note that contrary to the totalizing and authoritarian tendencies of Islamic authorities today, Islamic history and traditions reveal a vibrant competition between various schools of thought. There is *ijtihad* and *ijma* or decisions arrived by reasoning and consensus. Needless to say, law-making even in Islam had evolved through consensual and democratized means; in the modern world, this practice should continue even more. In Malaysia, there should be a return to constitutional principles — wherein Islam should be decentralized and come under the purview of traditional rulers and state governments. In Indonesia, while decentralization politics has led to the enforcement of many local-level *Syariah* laws, the climate of freedom of expression should be allowed to thrive. In both countries, all interest groups should be given a stake in determining through consensus, compromises and accommodations as to how Islam should be lived within a multi-religious and culturally-plural society.

Notes

1. Malaysia has three territories which come under federal purview — the Wilayah Persekutuan, Labuan and Putra Jaya. The Islamic enactments for these territories are passed by Parliament. Islamic laws for these territories are contained in the 1984 Federal Territory Enactment on the Administration of Islamic Law.
2. Musdah (2008) (slides given with permission from author).
3. For example in Section 21 of the *UU Pornografi*, it is written that: "Masyarakat dapat berperan serta dalam melakukan pencegahan terhadap pembuatan, penyebarluasan, dan penggunaan pornografi." [translated: "Society has a collective role in preventing the production, dissemination and the use of pornography."] See Rancangan Undang-Undang Republik Indonesia Tentang Pornografi; there are many websites posting the contents of the law, for example <http://tulisanperempuan.wordpress.com/2008/10/07/rancangan-undang-undang-republik-indonesia-tentang-pornografi/> (accessed 3 December 2008).
4. UNDP (nd, p. 48).
5. See Press Statement by SIS Forum Malaysia (Sisters in Islam), *Husbands May Misuse Amendments to Islamic Family Law Bill, Federal Territories, 2005*, 8 December 2005.
6. See Memorandum to Ahli Dewan Negara to Review the Islamic Family Law (Federal Territories) (Amendment), submitted by the Joint Action Group (JAG) on Gender Equality, 8 December 2005 <http://www.sistersinislam.org.my/index.php?option=com_content&task=view&id=686&Itemid=302> (accessed 16 December 2008).
7. Masjaliza (2008).
8. Musdah (2008).
9. Hayat (2008).

References

Ahmad Ibrahim. *Islamic Law in Malaya*. Singapore: Malaysian Sociological Research Institute Ltd., 1965.

Cammack, M. "Islamic Law in Indonesia's New Order". *The International and Comparative Law Quarterly* 38, no. 1 (January 1998): 53–73.

Fealy, Greg and Virginia Hooker. *Voices of Islam in Southeast Asia: A Contemporary Sourcebook*. Singapore: Institute of Southeast Asian Studies, 2006.

Gadis, Arivia. "Undang-Undang Pornografi dan Negara Moral". In *Kompas.com*, 1 December 2008 <http://entertainment.kompas.com/read/xml2008/12/01/02134110/undang-undang.pornografi.dan.negara.moral> (accessed 3 December 2008).

Hamidah Atan. "Enforcing Syariah Court Decisions". *New Sunday Times*, 15 June 2008, Prime News, p. 16.

Hayat Mansur. "UU Pornografi dan Pemilu 2009". In *Perspektif Online* <http://www.perspektif.net/indonesian/article.php?article_id=978> (accessed 3 December 2008).

Horowitz, D. "The Qur'an and the Common Law: Islamic Law Reform and the Theory of Legal Change". *The American Journal of Comparative Law* 42, no. 2 (Spring 1994): 543–80.

Kuek Ser Kuang Keng. "Hindu Man Gets Custody of Children". Malaysiakini.com, 3 May 2007 <http://juhamwilayah.wordpress.com/2007/06/04/wanita-india-yang-masuk-islam-tertipu/> (accessed 9 January 2009).

Masjaliza Hamzah. "Fatwas shouldn't be law". *The Nut Graph*, 28 November 2008 <http://www.thenutgraph.com/fatwas-shouldn't-be-law> (accessed 3 December 2008).

Mazwin Nik Anis. "Divorce Aid Proposal: Body to Help Kin Waits for Maintenance Order". *Sunday Star*, 15 June 2008, p. N14.

Musdah Mulia. "Interreligious Marriage (The Indonesian Case)". Powerpoint presentation at the Conference on Marriage, Culture and Poverty in Southeast Asia, Yogyakarta, Indonesia, 21 August 2008.

Siti Zubaidah Ismail. "Undang-Undang Prosedur Jenayah Syariah di Malaysia: Satu Penilaian". In *Mahkamah Syariah di Malaysia*, edited by A.H. Buang. Kuala Lumpur: Penerbit Universiti Malaya, 2006.

United Nations Development Programme (UNDP). "Access to Justice in Aceh: Making the Transition to Sustainable Peace and Development in Aceh" (n.d.) <http://www.undp.or.id/pubs/docs/Access to Justice.pdf.> (accessed 2 December 2008).

INDEX

www.ingramcontent.com/pod-product-compliance
Lightning Source LLC
Chambersburg PA
CBHW021539260326
41914CB00001B/76